BLOODY

HIST

SOUTHAMPTON

BLOODY BRITISH HISTORY

HISTORY

SOUTHAMPTON

PENNY LEGG

The
History
Press

For my favourite people:
My Joe, Thomas and his wife Joe, and Duncan

In Loving Memory of Mum:
Peggy Hale, 1937-2013

And Dad:
Tony Hale, 1937-2013

First published in 2013

The History Press
The Mill, Brimscombe Port
Stroud, Gloucestershire, GL5 2QG
www.thehistorypress.co.uk

British Library Cataloguing in Publication Data.
A catalogue record for this book is available from the British Library.

ISBN 978 0 7524 7110 5

Typesetting and origination by The History Press
Printed in Great Britain

CONTENTS

ACKNOWLEDGEMENTS

THIS LOOK AT the nastier bits of Southampton's history has been a real eye-opener to write. It is amazing what you find when you start digging! I could not have done it without the help of the following people, to whom I say a big, 'Thank you!'.

Cate Ludlow, my commissioning editor at The History Press, who had an idea for a new kind of history book series and who asked me to write one for Southampton – super!

Nicola Guy at The History Press, for her patience.

Brian Hooper and Jeff Henry from the website *Southampton in Song*, for their prompt and helpful advice and the use of songs from their CD of the same name.

The librarians at Woolston library, who are simply wonderful.

Iris Mardon, for her wonderful memories of wartime Southampton.

Pam Whittington, for her help when it was most needed.

The Local Studies Desk at Southampton Reference Library.

Last, but not least, my lovely husband, Joe, who patiently puts up with me when I am writing a book, secure in the knowledge that he will be able to fill me in on what I have missed in the present, while I have been busy delving into the past.

INTRODUCTION

WE HAVE ALL endured long and very boring history lessons, where dull facts and figures were drummed into us to the extent that we could regurgitate them at examination time. Most of this information was instantly forgotten the moment the ordeal was over. What was left was only the interesting stuff – the bits that caught our attention and, even more, stirred our imagination. Thus, we know forever what fate awaited each of Henry VIII's six wives (we can chant: divorced, beheaded, died, divorced, beheaded, survived); why the Black Death was so called (we can see the fleas riding in the fur of those rats and we shudder, knowing what was to come) and what caused the Great Fire of London (we wonder, horrified but fascinated, at the speed the fire spread through the capital, bringing its trail of death and destruction as it sped along). Most of us haven't a clue exactly when women got the vote, but we remember our lesson on the suffragette Emily Wilding Davison (1872–1913),

who threw herself under the King's horse, Anmer, on the Tattenham Corner turn of the Epsom Derby in 1913. The fractured skull and internal injuries that resulted from this encounter killed her four days later. In fact, it is the very nature of the fate of people and places that keep us interested, often riveted. It is no coincidence that the Tower of London, scene of unexplained deaths, executions and more, is a major tourist attraction.

Southampton is no different to other towns in Great Britain. It has a rich heritage of lively events, both happy and sad, that have shaped it into the city it is today. This book is not meant to be a history of the port. Instead, it is a book about pockets of the history of the city – the interesting bits; the bits that we will remember after reading them – the bloody bits!

Enjoy.

Penny Legg 2013

837

THE DANES ARE COMING!

RAIDING AND PLUNDERING!

England was a divided kingdom just waiting to be plundered and the Danes, part of the feared Norse Viking raiders, took full advantage.

Population growth was one of the deciding factors for the start of the raids. The need to find new areas to colonise, together with the desire for conquest and plunder, combined with advances in shipbuilding technology, led to the raids that saw Viking settlements springing up in East Anglia, Western Scotland, parts of Wales and southern Ireland. The raids began in 793 in Lindisfarne and, by the ninth century, had reached their peak.

The raiders came in by night, making defence difficult.

Viking raiders.

MARAUDERS AND SLAUGHTER!

In 837 Southampton was attacked, but the marauders were beaten back and the residents breathed a sigh of relief that their world had not been turned upside down by the fierce people from a strange land. The *Anglo-Saxon Chronicle* states that, '... Ealdorman Wulfheard (an Ealdorman is a high-ranking official charged with command of the army in place of the king) fought at Southampton against the crews of thirty-three ships, made a great slaughter there and had the victory ...'

Peace was not to last though. The Danes made repeated attacks on Wessex, the area of England below the Thames, wishing to expand on their holdings in East Anglia. In 871, Saxon King Ethelred and his brother Alfred defeated them in Berkshire but the Danes' reply was to defeat Ethelred's forces at Old Basing in Hampshire two weeks later. Ethelred died shortly after this battle, leaving the throne to Alfred.

Anyone gazing on Hamo Thorneycroft's splendid statue of King Alfred in Winchester will not fail to be impressed by Wessex's greatest leader, despite the most well-known story about him being that he burnt cakes. The

King Alfred.

statue was erected in 1899 and depicts him crowned, with his shield on his arm and with his sword upside down so that it resembles a cross, held aloft. He was a devout Christian, who happened to be a warrior king. He made Winchester his capital, but life was not quiet after Old Basing and for the next eight years he battled to keep his kingdom.

Peace came after the battle of Ethandun in 878, when the Danes were starved into submission in Chippenham. The Danish leader, Guthrum, converted to Christianity and he and Alfred agreed on a split of territory between them.

KILLING AND CAPTIVITY!

However, the Danes returned, and with a vengeance. In one of the versions of the *Anglo Saxon Chronicle* (Version C), it is stated that in 980 'Southampton was sacked by a naval force, and most of the citizens killed or taken captive ...' In Versions D and E, the year is given as 981 and further details are supplied; 'In this year there first came seven ships and ravaged Southampton.'

Alfred was under no illusions. After having to retake London from the ever-encroaching Danes in 886, he set about establishing shipyards, building ships larger than those that the Norsemen sailed in. The naval shipyard on the Itchen at Woolston was possibly one that was started in Alfred's time.

The new ships were engaged in a battle on the Solent in 897, when Alfred's force succeeded in defeating the invaders, who had brought along their wives and children to settle the area they wished to conquer.

OCCUPIED!

Alfred died in 901, but the threat from the Vikings was ever-present. In September 994, ninety-four Danish ships attacked London but were fought off. The surviving forces then 'did the greatest damage that ever any army could do, by burning, ravaging and slaying everywhere along the coast, and in Essex, Kent, Sussex and Hampshire,' (*Anglo Saxon Chronicle*). In desperation, King Ethelred the Unready paid bribes, 'tribute', and gave the marauders provisions on the condition that they promised to stop the 'harrying'. The *Anglo Saxon Chronicle* continues, 'And they then accepted that, and the whole army came then to Southampton and took winter quarters there; and they were paid 16,000 pounds in money'. The citizens of Southampton had to put up with their very unwelcome guests until Olaf Tryggvason, the Danish army's leader, promised on payment of gifts, that he would 'never come back to England in hostility.' Southampton, and the rest of the country, no doubt breathed a sigh of relief!

Southampton Water is said to be the place that Canute (Cnut, crowned King in Southampton in 1016, died 1035) sat on the beach and commanded the waves to stop advancing. When they lapped at his feet, Henry of Huntington (1080-*c.* 1160), the Archdeacon of the Diocese of Lincoln, states that he said, 'Let all men know how empty and worthless is the power of kings, for there is none worthy of the name, but He whom heaven, earth, and sea obey by eternal laws,' (*Historia Anglorum, or History of the English*). Under Canute's rule, England enjoyed peace and prosperity.

King Canute meeting Edmund Ironside.

THE NORMANS ARRIVE!

THE NORSEMEN

The Normans were descended from the Vikings, or Norsemen, who had been granted lands in northern France in 911 in return for their support in beating back further Viking raids on the area. They had had a close affinity with England since the marriage of England's King Aethelred II, 'the Unready' (968–1016) to Emma (*c*. 985–1052), the daughter of the Duke of Normandy, Richard III, 'the Fearless' (933–996). Their son, Edward the Confessor (1003/5–1066) became King of England in 1042, after a long period of living in Normandy. He was heavily influenced by the Norman supporters he installed in key positions at Court and in the Church to advise him. Thus, the Normans became involved with English political affairs and this was to have major consequences for the country when Edward died, childless and with no clear heir.

Coin of Edward the Confessor.

HAROLD, HARALD AND WILLIAM

Harold, Earl of Wessex, was proclaimed king but there were two foreign claimants to the throne to worry about. One was William of Normandy, who said that Edward had promised him the English throne, and that Harold had been present when he did so, and Harald Hardrada, also known as Harald III (1016–1066) of Norway, whose claim went back to Edward's predecessor, Harthacanute (*c*. 1018–1042), son of Canute (*c*. 985–1035). They, so Harald Hardrada would have it, had had a pact that if either of them died childless, the throne of the other would go to the survivor. As Harthacanute had done just that, the throne, he claimed, should be his. Either way, Harold was not going to have an easy time, as both these pretenders amassed armies to invade and forcibly seize the throne.

Harold spent the majority of his short reign worrying about the antics of his disaffected half-brother, Tostig Godwinson, who held a grudge after losing the Earldom of Northumbria. His fleet, recruited in Flanders, attacked ports along the south-east and east coasts, and waited with his militia army to rebuff William's expected invasion on the south coast. Both William and Harald Hardrada's invading forces arrived in England almost simultaneously but on different shores, miles from each other. Harold had sent many of his militia home on 8 September to bring in the harvest, so was left with a depleted following – just when he needed to be strong.

INVASION!

Harald Hardrada's invasion force consisted of more than 300 ships and 15,000 men. He meant business and was soon joined by Tostig and his men, throwing in his lot with the Scandinavians. After the battle of Fulford, in which Harald Hardrada had been victorious against troops led by Harold's supporters Morcar and Edwin, morale was high amongst the Norwegian force, so it was a surprise to be attacked by Harold and the troops he had recruited on an heroic 185-mile dash from the south coast to Stamford Bridge in Yorkshire. They met on 25 September and the resulting battle was bloody, all the more so because it was a hot day and the Norwegian forces, not expecting to be fighting, had taken off their protective chainmail shirts. The fighting was so fierce that at the end of it both Harald Hardrada and Tostig were dead, and only twenty-four ships were needed to carry the survivors home to Norway.

The toll had been hard on Harold's army, too. They needed time to recover and heal their wounds. However, this was not possible, as Harold now needed to repel William. He left part of his army in the north and marched the rest south. In the meantime, William and his forces arrived in England at Pevensey on 28 September. They immediately began to make themselves at home, building a wooden castle in Hastings, the first of many all over the country, to use as a base. They then set out to subdue the local population, and waited for Harold to realise they were there.

OUTCLASSED

The decisive battle commenced on 14 October 1066. Harold had hoped to take William by surprise, but the Norman was wily and had spies out ready to spot his enemy's advancing men. William also had archers and cavalry, while Harold had only men on foot. Although Harold had everything to lose, he was outclassed. Harold and a large number of his men were slain. The prevailing theory is that Harold died after being hit in the eye by an arrow, a view backed up by the depiction of Harold on the twelfth-century Bayeux Tapestry. There was much confusion as to exactly how Harold died, and this may or may not be the truth. William, though, had won his first, and most important, victory in his conquest of England.

The Battle of Hastings.

WELCOMED WITH OPEN ARMS?

If William thought that he would then be welcomed with open arms, he was mistaken. He would have to fight his way to London, eventually to be crowned king in Westminster Abbey on 25 December.

A GOOD DEAL

The Norman conquest of England in 1066 could not have been a better deal for Southampton. After all, settlers from another country will always want to keep up their links with their mother country, won't they? This is precisely what the conquerors wanted, and they soon used Southampton as a major transit port from Winchester, England's capital, to Normandy. The town prospered.

Southampton was a thriving centre of commerce and trade long before the Normans arrived. The earliest known coins produced at the town's mint came from the reign of Athelstan (924–939). Coins continued to be minted in the town until Cnut's era (1016–1035).

FRENCH QUARTER

There had been a French quarter in the town since before the conquest. Twenty years later, it is mentioned in Domesday Book of 1086 that there were sixty-five men of French origin and thirty-one of English descent in the town. Residents lived in separate areas, with the French settled in the aptly named French Street, in the south-west of the town, and the English living in English Street, south of the Bargate. St Michael's Church (St Michael being the patron saint of Normandy) is in the centre of

William the Conqueror.

the old French section of town, and it has been dated to 1070. Originally built in a cruciform shape, it was extended in the fourteenth and fifteenth centuries. The Norman structure included the tower, which is still standing. The font is one of six dating from 1170 and is made of black marble, which came from Tournai in Belgium. Another can be seen in Winchester Cathedral. Its full title is the Church of St Michael the Archangel, and it is the oldest building still actively being used for its original purpose in Southampton.

SOUTHAMPTON CASTLE

The Normans were great builders, and examples of their skill can still be seen standing all over the country. Their Romanesque architecture featured massive proportions, and rounded arches over doorways and windows. Eager to make sure that their new lands were not taken from them, they built many fortifications in England, including castles. In Southampton they built a wooden motte and bailey structure, first mentioned as a *munito* or

---

In 1968, archaeologists excavating whilst Castle Way was being built found more than they expected in the rubbish tip they were examining at the corner of Broad Lane and High Street. A hoard of Norman coins – *derniers* – dating from 1030 was unearthed.

---

fortified residence in 1153 (Rance). It was in the north-west part of town and overlooked the River Test, an important waterway at the time. It is shown prominently on John Speed's 1612 map of Southampton. The bailey, an enclosed courtyard, surrounded the motte, or raised earthworks. On the top of the 45ft motte, was a wooden keep or fortified tower. A stone castle was introduced in the twelfth century, when Henry II took an interest in renovating and improving the site. Some of his improvements of 1150 and 1160 can still be seen today, including the large hall built abutting the cliff and the Castle Vault for storing wine. At the time, Southampton was an important port, and the wine trade was of particular note.

PLUNDER

Richard II built a new keep with four turrets between 1378 and 1380, as a reaction to threats of invasion from France. He also refurbished the castle, which had been falling into disrepair

as locals had plundered it for its stone. Southampton Castle became one of the first castles in the country to be fitted with a cannon in 1382.

Speed's map shows the mound with the turreted castle atop it. By 1618 though, the castle was in ruins and it was sold into private hands. A windmill was erected on the motte and some of the stone was later used to repair the town walls. In the nineteenth century a gothic mansion, Lansdowne House, was built on the site, using stone still remaining from the medieval structure. The house is described in Revd J. S. Davies' *A History of Southampton* as 'castellated' and 'of brick and stucco'. This was short-lived; its owner, the Marquis of Lansdowne, elected a town burgess in 1805, and died in 1809. His successor was his half-brother, who sold the house, for building materials, and the freehold to the land. The mansion was demolished in 1815/9. After that time, the site was levelled and built upon. Although there are glimpses of the old castle still visible, much has now been covered over by roads and housing.

1173

LEPROSY IN SOUTHAMPTON

UNCLEAN!

This was the Victorian view of leprosy, the disease that has been with man since at least the fourth century BC. It was long thought to be a curse from the gods, and priests were left to treat it as best they could. Members of the same family often had leprosy, and so it was considered to be hereditary. Avoiding those with the disease also meant avoiding infection, and so suffers often had to ring a bell to alert the uninfected and give them time to move out of the way. However, the bell was also used to alert those wishing to give alms to the sick, so it had a dual purpose. Those with leprosy often lived together in colonies; these were frequently situated on or near main

Christ curing lepers.

thoroughfares, meaning that the lepers had maximum chance to beg for alms from passing travellers.

Scientists now think that leprosy is spread either by respiratory droplet infection or from environmental conditions. It is also sometimes already present in a person's genetics. It can take up to five years from infection to the first appearance of symptoms.

SEVERE PAIN

There are two forms of leprosy. The mild form of the disease is tuberculoid, or paucibacillary, leprosy. This causes red patches on the skin, which have less touch sensation. Skin stiffens and dries out, and muscles in the hands and feet weaken. There is severe pain and the possibility of the loss of sight, fingers and toes. Nerves in the elbow and knee enlarge.

NASAL COLLAPSE

Lepromatous or mulitbacillary leprosy is the severe form of the disease. Symptoms include a symmetrical skin rash on the face, ears, wrists, elbows, knees and buttocks. The rash can be light or dark, flat or raised, large or small. The disease

Nowadays, although overall the disease has declined globally, leprosy is becoming of increasing concern as it is developing drug resistant forms. India accounts for the highest percentage of cases in the twenty-first century.

A group of lepers.

also causes thinning of the eyebrows and eyelashes, thickened facial skin, bloody nose, nasal stuffiness and nose collapse, laryngitis, swelling of the lymph nodes in the groin and armpits, scarring of the testes leading to infertility, and enlargement of the male breasts. This truly gruesome disease can also lead to blindness, loss of fingers or toes and arthritis. It was no wonder that the healthy took pains to keep away from the sufferers. Pity was also a powerful motive in alms giving.

LE MAUDELYNE

In Southampton, the Hospital of St Mary Magdalene, called Le Maudelyne on early town accounts, was founded *c.* 1172. The Pipe Roll for that time shows a charge of £1 3*s* 2*d* as allowance for land given to Southampton's lepers. The town burgesses had founded the hospital from their own pockets. In 1179 it was assigned to the Priory of St Denys.

The Burgesses appointed the master of the hospital, but in the reign of Edward I this duty was taken over by the Crown, much to the annoyance of the town dignitaries, who saw it as a loss of privilege.

SIR BEVOIS OF SOUTHAMPTON

Real hero or folklore legend?

THE CITY OF Southampton abounds with references to the legend of Sir Bevois (Bevis); his love Josian; Ascupart, the giant who became his page; and the lions who guarded Josian. Take a wander around the city and you will come across Bevois Street, Josian Walk and Ascupart Street in the aptly named Kingsland. Bevois Valley Road cuts through Bevois Valley, with its landmark sculpture *Shere* by Eilis O'Connel – a symbol of the magic sword Bevois gave to Josian and meant to represent justice. There is a Bevois Park, and lions guard the Bargate.

The wooden lions were gilded at great expense when Queen Elizabeth I came to Southampton. She was particularly interested in peace-loving Josian, who was such a fit mate for Bevois that lions chose to guard her, rather than devour her.

Clearly, Southampton has claimed Bevois as its own. It is said that Bevois was the first Earl of Southampton, although this honour actually went to Thomas Wriothesley (1505–1550).

WHO WAS BEVOIS?

According to Veronica Tippetts ('The Triumph of Fiction over Fact' published in *Life to the Full Magazine*),

Tudor monarchs enjoyed the Anglo-Norman version of Bevois' story, written to flatter William d'Aubigny, the first Earl of Arundel (*c.* 1109–1176). However, Viktoria Turner, in her paper 'Legends, Lions, and Virgins: The Legend of Sir Bevois of Southampton' tells us that, 'an open mind should be kept as to whether the original pre-Norman version of the legend was based on fact or not.' Those who do believe, and who wish to know what their heroes may have looked like, should travel to St Peter's Church in Curdbridge. There, high up on the Victorian tower are gargoyles, dating from 1894. Bevois is depicted in chain mail and in the act of drawing his sword; his beautiful love Josian gazes benignly down on all who pass, as does Ascupart and Arundel, Bevois' horse.

Was he real? The *This is Hampshire* website says not: 'There was no real Sir Bevois.' However, what we know about Bevois is quite a lot. Much of this information has been passed down from Anglo-Nordic romantic poetry dating from the twelfth century, which itself stemmed from an earlier, and now lost, Middle English version. Michael Drayton (1563–1631) also tells the story in his *Poly-Olbion* in Song ii, published in 1612.

MURDER

Like all good folktales, there is much blood and gore along the way. The tale is told of Sir Bevois, the son of Sir Guy of Hampton (now Southampton) and an unnamed mother, who was the daughter of the King of Scotland. Old Sir Guy had married a much younger bride and she promptly took a lover, whom she later asked to murder her husband. This grisly deed done, the two of them married and settled down to live happily ever after.

They might have been happy, but little Sir Bevois was not. Turner cites *The History of Hampshire* to tell us that at the age of seven, Sir Bevois is said to have 'cudgelled his step-father almost to death'. Clearly, the little boy held a grudge for the murder of his father. He was not going to be given a second chance to do away with his murderous step-father, as his mother took matters into her own hands. Her maternal instincts were obviously not her primary concern, as she promptly sold her son into slavery.

SLAVERY

In this time of the Crusades, it was to Islamic Armenia that Sir Bevois was taken, where he was resold to Ermyn, the Armenian king (mentioned by Chaucer in *The Canterbury Tales*). Time passed, and his exploits became legendary. He is said to have escaped his captivity, fought his enemies and is remembered for the killing of a wild boar, which had been causing chaos in the area. In true heroic fashion, his mighty sword Mortglay (a superb phallic symbol, as Tippetts points out), which was said to have magical

properties, and his horse, Hirondelle (also known as Arundel the Swallow) were part of the growing folklore, too.

LIONS

Ermyn had a beautiful daughter, Josian (Joisyan). Sir Bevois fell in love with her at first sight. As legend would have it, he had been warned not to marry a woman who was not pure; he was also told that his wife had to be a king's daughter. Josian had been married to Yvor of Mombraunt for seven unhappy, virginal years. According to Ralph Hanna (*London Literature, 1300–1380*), Yvor was the villain of the piece. At one point in the story, he chains up Arundel because the horse refuses to be ridden by any other than Sir Bevois, thus showing that even a horse can tell the difference between a hero and a cad when he sees one!

Sir Bevois carries Josian off and leaves her sheltering in a cave, with her servant, Boniface. While he is away, two lions feast on the luckless Boniface, but as Josian is both a king's daughter and virtuous, they are unable to touch her and so sit outside the cave, one on either side of the entrance, guarding her. Sir Bevois, recognising the danger they represent, promptly slays them on his return.

ATTACK!

Sir Bevois found himself with a squire, Ascapart, after being attacked by him on an Armenian seashore. Josian, ever the peacemaker, stepped between them and stopped Sir Bevois from killing him, saying that Ascapart should serve Sir Bevois instead.

Arundel Castle overlooks the River Arun in West Sussex. The Earl of Arundel, Roger de Montgomery, built it at the end of the eleventh century. Today it is the home of the Duke and Duchess of Norfolk.

The Arundel Tower dates from 1290 and may well have been named after Sir John Arundel, a governor of Southampton Castle.

REVENGE!

Back in Southampton, both Sir Bevois and Ascapart were christened in Southampton Water. After this, Sir Bevois and Josian were married.

The urge to come back to his own land was fuelled by the fact that Sir Bevois wanted to avenge his father's death

The ruined keep of Arundel Castle, supposedly built by Sir Bevois.

and to reclaim his lands. In true grisly medieval style, he is said to have driven his mother to leap to her death from the top of a high tower; he then boiled her liver in a giant cauldron to make dog meat.

Other tales about Sir Bevois are that he built Arundel Castle in Sussex, while another states that he built the Arundel Tower on the town's defensive walls. Whichever building he is supposed to have created, he named it after his warrior steed.

DEATH

As with all great folk heroes, there is mystery about Sir Bevois's death. When he realised he was dying, he is supposed to have gone to the top of the Arundel Tower and thrown Mortglay, his magical sword, as far as he could. It travelled a distance of two miles, and the sword landed in two pieces. It is here that Sir Bevois is supposed to be buried, on land now known as Bevois Mount.

Romantics however like the idea of Sir Bevois and Josian dying in each other's arms, as happens in another version of the end of the Sir Bevois' tale.

THE CONVENT OF FRIARS MINOR

POVERTY

Franciscan friars came to Southampton in the thirteenth century, probably around 1233. They took their name from St Francis of Assisi and were part of a new order, calling themselves 'Friars Minor' as they were (according to *A History of Southampton*) the 'youngest and humblest of the religious orders'. They wore grey habits and deliberately lived in poverty, despite efforts by the town burgesses to improve their living standards. The burgesses' main contribution was the building of a smart stone friary, which was pulled down soon after because it was felt to be too luxurious by Brother Albert of Pisa, minister-provincial of England. A new, less grand and far less comfortable building replaced it. The Southampton friary, on the corner of English Street and Broad Lane, to the north of St Julian's hospital (God's House Hospital), was probably the earliest of the Minorite order established in England. The site of the friary was deliberate, as the friars were set up to look after the sick and the poor, and so they sought out the neediest parts of a town in which to base themselves.

Southampton residents had good reason to be grateful to the Friars Minor. Nicholas de Barbeflet offered the use of a

A member of Friars Minor. (Courtesy of Thomas Fisher Rare Book Library, University of Toronto)

spring in Shirley to supply their premises with water. In 1304 this offer was taken up and by 1309 various benefactors had assisted to allow work to go ahead on a conduit-head, a protective, domed stone building, and pipework to bring water over one mile to the friary. It was also piped for public use at All Saints' Church, Holy Rood Church and God's House Hospital. When the pipes fell into disrepair in the thirteenth century, the town corporation took over the running of them.

When the friary was closed (1538) and sold off (1545) as part of the Dissolution of the Monasteries, a curious book was found in the library. It was written in poetical metre and was a comprehensive work on the Philosopher's Stone, supposedly found at the friary. The Philosopher's Stone, as anyone who has read *Harry Potter* will know, was the prize of alchemy, a substance of seemingly amazing possibilities – turning base metals into gold or silver or being an elixir of life, able to rejuvenate or give immortality. Alchemists had sought the Philosopher's Stone for centuries, without success. Now, it had allegedly been discovered in a friary in Southampton!

An illustration from a guide on how to make the Philosopher's Stone.

1321

PIRATES!

DECAYED DEFENCES

Southampton had been lax in building and looking after its defences, which began simply as an earthen bank with a palisade and a ditch. Southampton Castle was allowed to decay, and in 1246, there is a record of the Southampton population being fined for 'selling timber, lead and stone from that demolished building' (*Southampton: An Illustrated History*). By 1286 though, a murage grant – a toll taken specifically towards a particular project – was given to rebuild the castle, and other such grants were used to start building works on town defences. However, the sea defences were not improved, and rich houses opened on to the quays and the water.

SHIPPING AT RISK!

Shipping was at risk from pirates during the fourteenth century, particularly while on the Gascon run, trading between Southampton and Gascony in France. This was an important trade route for wine, some of which was destined for Southampton's consumption, while the rest was for the London markets or the King's cellars. In 1321 the men of Winchelsea came calling on Southampton.

WINCHELSEA MEN

Winchelsea men had a notorious reputation. The port was recorded as the third most important in the south, after London and Southampton. The mariners based in the town were legally privateers during times of war, as were seafarers based in other ports. A fifth of the resulting booty seized by the privateers went straight into the Crown's purse. Unfortunately for

Walking the plank.

A portrait of a typical pirate. Behind him is a burning ship.

Southampton, in peacetime these men were pirates, which were, officially at least, illegal. As pirates they did not mind which country's ships they attacked –

foreign or otherwise – and they happily terrorised the South Coast in the thirteenth and fourteenth centuries.

In 1290, after years of persecution and massacres in London and York, all Jews were expelled from England. A Winchelsea pirate ship stopped one ship, filled with the unfortunate expellees. The Jewish passengers were forced off their vessel and left to drown on a sandbank, while their ship was plundered.

On 30 September 1321, the Winchelsea men daringly attacked Southampton ships. Thirty Winchelsea ships came to Southampton that day. They burnt fifteen ships to begin with. The town burgesses, appalled by the destruction, tried to head off further trouble with the offer of two new ships if they left and did no further damage. This offer was refused and the raiders burnt two more ships before finally leaving.

1338

THE SACK OF SOUTHAMPTON

DIRE PERIL!

The destructive raid on Southampton by the Winchelsea pirates in 1321 showed where the town was vulnerable. By 1338, a fateful date in the area's history, there was still not enough money to strengthen the sea defences. Southampton didn't know it, but it was in dire peril.

DESTRUCTION

On Sunday 4 October, a fleet of Genoese and French ships arrived in Southampton bent on destruction, the like of which would change the port's fortunes overnight.

Fifty ships sailed into the West Quay area of town at about nine in the morning – just as many of the folk were at church. The sea defences left the area virtually unprotected and the enemy fleet, all under the pay of the King of France, took full advantage.

The raiders were led by Sir Hugh Quiriel, Sir Peter Bahucet and Barbenoir, described as 'admirals and conductors of their fleet' by Sir John Froissart, writing in the fourteenth century. He describes the raid: 'Normans, Picards and Spaniards entered the town, pillaged it, killed many, deflowered maidens and forced wives ...' Many of the town's people killed were massacred in the eleventh-century St Michael's church, which was badly damaged by fire.

St Michael's church.

Southampton's south shore – enemy ships sailed into this harbour, bent on destruction. The land has since been reclaimed.

'SPOYLED AND RAYSYD'

The inhabitants of the area fled, leaving the town 'spoyled and raysyd by French pyrates' (Leland, *Itinerary*, pub.1769). The invaders stayed overnight, which gave the men of the town time to gather reinforcements and mount a counter-attack the next morning, by which time the ships had been loaded with large amounts of plunder, most notably wool and wine. The ensuing battle left 300 of the enemy dead.

RANCON!

The oft-repeated story of one of the dead, the son of the King of Sicily, gives an example of the ferocity of the fighting. He was in mortal combat with a local unnamed farmer and was losing the fight. He cried, 'Rancon,' expecting the custom of highborn men to be taken prisoner for ransom to be honoured. He had however, reckoned without local misunderstanding. The farmer mistook his cry for that of the patriotic, and in the circumstances, defiant 'Francon', and clubbed him to death. Revd J. Silvester Davies (*A History of Southampton*, 1883) quotes the farmer as saying, 'Yea, I know thou art a Francon, and therefore thou shalt die.'

The invading fleet was driven back, setting fire to buildings on their retreat back

Warships of the era.

to their ships, and the town was left to lick its wounds.

As a result of the sack of Southampton, Edward III, furious that such an attack had been mounted on a large and prestigious port, appointed Richard FitzAlan, 10th Earl of Arundel, to enquire into the circumstances of the attack. He wanted to name and shame those who had neglected their duty to the town.

Edward III

Southampton was never the same after the sack. The wool trade declined as merchants transferred their business to safer ports, such as Bristol. So many of the tenement buildings were damaged that the rents given to religious concerns such as the hospital at God's House, which owned many of them, declined to such a point that it took over a century for them to recover to their former level.

MARTIAL LAW

What amounted to martial law was the order of the day for the town's inhabitants following the sack. If the burgesses could not defend the town, then the king would see to it that soldiers could. He moved overseers in to keep the town on his behalf. He paid for men-at-arms and archers to be ready to defend the town, and he ordered that a stout defensive wall enclose the town.

SACK OF SOUTHAMPTON BY ROB SIBTHORPE

In thirteen hundred and thirty-eight on the fourth day of October
There came a fleet of fifty galleys upon Southampton Water,
They landed at the Gravel, close by the western shore,
Came rushing up old Bull Street, into the town did pour.

So come you bold Southampton men, listen to the call,
You'd better be quick when you build your walls
Or you'll do no building at all.

They slew the children in the streets and the women in the houses,
They stabbed the holy congregation running from St Michael's;
They filled the town with fire, and filled the men with dread,
The burgesses, like cowards, to the countryside had fled.

So come you bold …

All that day they wreaked their will with fire and sword and dagger,
While the men of old Southampton outside the town did gather;
Their numbers swelled by volunteers from the countryside all round,
'At dawn we'll be back and we'll take revenge for the sacking of our town.'

So come you bold …

By dawn the French and Spaniards and the other bold invaders
Slept exhausted from a day and night of evil favours;
When suddenly the English came storming through the town,
They drove the pirates to the sea and they cut the stragglers down.

So come you bold …

In thirteen hundred and thirty-eight on the fourth day of October
There came a fleet of fifty galleys upon Southampton Water;
And for a while they held the town, but gave the town away,
Leaving homes and lives destroyed that flourished yesterday.

So come you bold Southampton men, listen to the call,
You'd better be quick when you build your walls
Or you'll do no building, you'll do no building,
You'll do no building at all.

1348–1351

THE PESTILENCE

DECAY, DEATH AND DESTRUCTION

Even after all that had befallen Southampton, the defences for the town were still in a bad way years after the sack of the town. Allegations of corruption were made in 1341 and there were further enquiries about the decay and neglect of the earthworks over the next twenty years. By then, death and destruction had reached Southampton from an entirely different source.

THE BLACK DEATH

Plague was no respecter of class, wealth, gender or position. Wherever it went, it killed. As it spread it left devastation in its wake – sometimes entire villages succumbed.

The dance of death, leading Southampton to its end.

RING, A RING OF ROSES ...

There are several forms of plague. Pneumonic plague gave its victims a fever. They spat blood and their body became marked with small black pustules, giving rise to the name 'The Black Death'. It was the more infectious of the two versions, and it was almost always fatal. It infected the respiratory system and was spread by droplet infection – by coughing, sneezing or by kissing. The nursery song, *Ring, A Ring o' Roses* perhaps remembers this form of the disease. It was a quick killer. The sufferer was often bed ridden for two or three days and dead by the third or fourth day. The disease enjoyed the cold of the wintertime.

INFECTED RATS

Unlike pneumonic plague, fleas from infected rats spread bubonic plague. The symptoms once again included a fever, but sufferers of bubonic plague also had severe boils or abscesses and enlarged lymph glands, called buboes – hence the name for this form of the disease. These appeared on the groin, armpits and neck. This form was deadly, but more sufferers survived it than those with the pneumonic plague. It was especially prevalent in the warmer summer months. The septicaemic version of bubonic

---

We all know the nursery rhyme *Ring A Ring o' Roses*:

> Ring, a ring of roses,
> A pocket full of posies,
> Atishoo, atishoo,
> We all fall down.

It has long been asserted that this is a song about the plague. Small children dance around in a circle as they sing it, mime sneezing and then fall to the floor at the end. This would seem to mimic the symptoms of the pneumonic version of the disease and its aftermath. However, the rhyme was not published until 1881 in *Mother Goose* by Kate Greenaway. The last two lines then are written:

> Hush! Hush! Hush! Hush!
> We're all tumbled down.

In this version, it loses its significance to the pestilence. There are other versions, too, for example, with 'Ashes! Ashes!' as the third line, and it is also in languages other than English, which do not have relevance to the plague. Some folklorists therefore reject it completely as a song associated with the plague.

There is debate as to when it was written. Although it was first published in 1881, there were versions known to be older. Could it be that the cost of printing was too great before the first publication for it to be considered worthy of the investment, or is it just a meaningless children's rhyme that serious printers did not consider as deserving of publication?

---

plague was the quickest killer – the blood-borne bacteria killed in hours.

THE PLAGUE

The plague, probably the bubonic form spread by rats, hit England via the South Coast, possibly the port at Southampton or several ports simultaneously, brought in by trading vessels between June and August 1348. Henry Knighton, the Canon of St Mary's Leicester, writing in the late fourteenth century, wrote at length about the effects of 'The Black Death'. He said, 'For there is no memory of a mortality so severe and so savage from the time of Vortigern, king of the Britons, in whose time, as Bede says, the living did not suffice to bury the dead.'

Tom Beaumont James has studied the effects of plague in Hampshire (*The Black Death in Hampshire, 1999*). He mentions that by October 1348 there was a noticeable increase in the mortality rate in Hampshire. By 1349, the disease was rampaging through the county. In 1349 there were no less than three vicars appointed to the parish of Holy Rood.

Knighton goes further, 'At this same time there was so great a lack of priests everywhere that many windowed churches had no divine services, no Masses, matins, vespers, sacraments, and sacramentals.' Such was the suffering and death toll that the Church became worried about loss of faith and ordered sermons on resurrection to be given.

In 1349, during the height of the Black Death, there were no less than three vicars appointed to the parish of Holy Rood. The church was ruined during the Southampton Blitz in 1940.

In 1351, the town successfully negotiated a reduction in its fee farm, the annual sum due to the Exchequer in return for the king allowing the farmer to administer the borough, and its revenue streams in particular. This was said to be due to poverty because of the effects of the pestilence.

After the plague had died down, the landscape was never the same again. Peasants could be choosier about the land they wished to tenant, much land was sold and generally the masses who survived enjoyed a higher standard of living than before the disease arrived. Conversely, those higher up the class scale were poorer, having been brought to understand that their wealth did not shield them from suffering, or of the effects of such a catastrophic pandemic.

So numerous were the dead that the effect on rents was profound. Tenants were simply not there to pay them, and so they declined or ceased altogether, causing great problems for years to come. For those who lived, pay generally increased and profiteering from the labour shortage was rife.

That it took so long to do anything about Southampton's defences during this time may simply be down to the fact that so many people died. In 1377, there were approximately 1,600 people in Southampton, down from the roughly 2,500-2,800 figures of pre-plague times.

1415

TREASON!

THE SOUTHAMPTON PLOT

There is no doubt about it. The English and the French had hated each other for many centuries, and much blood was shed on both sides during this time. By the reign of Henry V (1413–1422), England was getting ready to invade France, and the port of Southampton was the place the English forces were to set sail from. First though, Henry had the small matter of treason to deal with.

King Richard II (1367–1400) had been deposed in 1399. He was the last of the Plantagenet kings. His heir, through his grandmother Philippa de Hainault (1314–1369), wife of King Edward III (1312–1377), had been Edmund Mortimer, the fifth Earl of March (1391–1425). Henry IV (1367–1413) had had problems

with several uprisings by those still loyal to Richard, who had been angered by the change in royal direction. He had kept Mortimer captive to ensure that he would be no trouble. When Henry V (1386–1422) succeeded his father, he set Mortimer free. Mortimer was allowed to return to his estates and, by all reports, he and the new king were on good terms.

However, others were not to be put off their efforts at stopping the new royal line. Mortimer's brother-in-law and cousin Richard, Earl of Cambridge (1385–1415) and two other conspirators, Henry, Lord Scrope of Masham (c.1370–1415) and Sir Thomas Grey of Heton (1384–1415) plotted the assassination of Henry V. They meant to replace him with Edmund Mortimer.

Visitors to the Red Lion Public House are sometimes startled by the various 'inhabitants' of the pub. The building has a cellar dating from 1148 and the exterior has Tudor beams. A procession of mournful people is allegedly sometimes seen leaving the Red Lion and heading toward the Bargate, a few hundred yards down the road. These are believed to be the Southampton Plot conspirators being led to their executions at the Bargate, just along the road. Inside the pub, a former barmaid sometimes makes an appearance. She is aged about sixty and is visible from the knees upwards. The Haunted Southampton Limited paranormal investigation company has conducted research at the pub and recorded unexplained activity all over the building.

Mortimer was informed of the plot and decided that the king should be told, thus saving his own life by turning in the disloyal trio.

GUILTY!

The three conspirators were rounded up and sent for trial on 2 August at the Red Lion Public House, in what has become known as the 'Court' or 'Trial' Room. Sir Thomas Grey was tried by jury first, found guilty – they had all confessed – and executed. According to Revd J. Silvester Davies he was 'led on foot from the Watergate to the North Gate (Bargate), outside which he was beheaded.'

His head was put on display at Newcastle upon Tyne. The other two were tried by their peers – led by the Duke of Clarence – at Southampton on 5 August and then also executed at the Bargate. Lord Scrope's head was sent to be displayed at York, and the Earl of Cambridge's body was buried in the chapel of God's House Hospital.

Henry V then went off to wage the wars that would end in victory at Agincourt in October 1415, which was the first step in the battle to retrieve French possessions.

The Red Lion was the scene of the trial of the Southampton Plot conspirators in 1415. The plot was to assassinate King Henry V and replace him with Edmund Mortimer, Fifth Earl of March. A mournful procession of ghostly figures moving towards the Bargate, the place of execution, is sometimes seen leaving the pub.

Henry died on 31 August 1422. If he had lived two months longer, he would have succeeded Charles VI and been crowned King of France. Mortimer was to die of plague in Ireland in 1425.

The Bargate was the scene of the executions of Richard, Earl of Cambridge (1385 – 1415), Henry, Lord Scrope of Masham (c.1370 – 1415) and Sir Thomas Grey of Heton (1384 – 1415), the Southampton Plot conspirators. The Bargate, formerly known as the Northgate, is reputed to be haunted. Researchers have investigated repeated reports of strange happenings in the building.

1417

GOD'S HOUSE TOWER

THE GATEHOUSE

There were numerous gates in the town walls in medieval Southampton. The Saltmarsh (or South) Gate opened out onto marshland, but also gave access to the newly built Town Quay. It is still standing at the junction of Winkle Street and Town Quay today.

The tower, part of the gatehouse, was originally named after the nearby St Julian's hospital, known as God's House Hospital, founded in 1168. The three-storey tower itself dates from 1417, when a two-storey gallery was also added to the gatehouse.

GUNPOWDER AND SHOT!

God's House Tower is remarkable for being one of the first purpose-built artillery fortifications in Britain. It housed gunpowder and shot on the ground floor and the firing platform was on the roof. There were eight gun ports. The Town Gunner was in charge of all. He had the job of making the gunpowder and the gunshot, and keeping the cannon in good repair.

The Town Gunner was the highest paid town official of his day. In 1457, according to the Steward's Book for that year (cited in *A History of Southampton*), he was paid 6*d* a day for his duties. Why so much? The year had previously seen French raids on Sandwich, during which the town was burnt. Southampton did not wish to have the same fate. The Steward's Book records the lengths the town went to to make sure the defences at God's House Tower were ready for the French should they come calling, as they did to Sandwich. They list everything from the 'hoggeshed to put in gonepowder' to the number of days' work Richard Carpenter put in (thirteen) 'in stokking of the gonnes'. The book also mentions that the first affray was by candlelight. By 1512, the Town Gunner was paid a yearly salary of 26*s* 8*d* (approximately £1.33) and 'a gown', no doubt a livery or uniform that enabled him to be identified in his official role. He also received additional payments for days when he made gunpowder – this was clearly danger money as the science was unpredictable!

The town gunner also had the responsibility of defending the sluice gates that allowed water in to the moat. The water ran the mill that was under the tower.

1420

THE *GRACE DIEU*

THE ROYAL NAVY HITS TOWN!

Naval shipbuilding in and around Southampton was once a thriving industry. The Royal Navy had been reduced to just one barge in 1410, but by 1419, the need for more ships with which to fight the French had resulted in shipbuilding moving from London to Southampton, and the Royal Navy basing itself in the port. The number of ships blossomed to thirty-six vessels, reflecting the need for a fleet when living on an island in times of war. The victory at the Battle of Agincourt had resulted in England owning lands in France, and Southampton was a more convenient port to sail to France from than Greenwich. Shipbuilders could also benefit from the proximity of the trees within the New Forest for use in constructing the ships.

The name of William Soper (*c.* 1390s-1459) was one that was prominent in fifteenth-century shipbuilding circles,

as he was both a burgess of Southampton (and mayor twice, in 1416 and 1424) and Clerk (or Keeper) of His Majesty's Ships from 1420 until 1442. He was also elected to the House of Commons eleven times between 1414 and 1449.

The navy was expensive. Henry V waged wars that cost a fortune, so any captured shipping was welcome. One of Soper's own vessels assisted in the capture of the Castilian merchant ship *Santa Clara* in 1414. The prize was brought back to Southampton and Soper received the king's commission to refit her for service in the English navy. The *Santa Clara* became the *Holy Ghost*.

Many of the ships in the Royal Navy were too small to fight the huge carracks, the three- or four-masted forerunner of the galleon, operated by the Genoese (allies of the French).

In 1416, Soper was involved in the biggest shipbuilding project thus far conceived (it would remain so for another 200 years) when the *Grace Dieu* and

---

Henry V died in debt and his fleet of ships had to be sold off or mothballed. All but four of the ships, the largest, were disposed of and the rest, apart from the *Grace Dieu*, slowly rotted or were later sold.

---

two ballingers (small seagoing ships with a shallow draught, built without a forecastle and usually with at least thirty oars for use in sheltered areas) were built. The *Grace Dieu* was a massive 200ft by 45ft (approximately 61m by 14m) and 1,400 tons (over double the size of the *Marie Rose*). She was clinker built; that is, built by overlapping planks of wood, and sat about 52ft (roughly 16m) above the waterline. To build her, Soper had to have a special dock erected near Town Quay. Labour was recruited from miles around – as far away as Devon and Cornwall – and she took two years to complete.

Soper supervised the *Grace Dieu*'s construction in the town and then moved her to be fitted out on the River Hamble. Here he had two giant store houses built, and erected a wooden tower at the river mouth to give protection against raiding French vessels. She was fitted with at least three cannon and would also have carried archers and soldiers aboard.

The *Grace Dieu* had one major disadvantage – she needed a huge crew (250 men) to sail her and it is here that the answer to her limited use may be found.

MUTINY

There seems to be only one record of her actually sailing, and this voyage is not remembered positively. In 1420, she was part of an expedition to 'keep the seas' (Rance) and was commanded by the 12th Earl of Devon, Hugh de Courteney (1389–1422). Soon after leaving Southampton, there was a mutiny on board just off Spithead in bad weather and the *Grace Dieu* had to put into St Helens on the Isle of Wight.

Shipbuilding was to be revived in Southampton from the seventeenth to the twentieth centuries. There was a boom following the 1698 survey of Southampton Water by Edmund Bumner, the Surveyor of the Navy. The small shipyard at Northam, on the River Itchen, established in 1693, produced its first 60-gun vessel in 1694, the Sunderland. Soon, there were shipyards at Chapel, Redbridge and Eling. In 1904, Thornycroft took over the shipyard at Woolston, owned by Nordey Carney & Co., and proceeded to make naval vessels. This eventually shut in 2004, bringing an end to naval shipbuilding in Southampton.

THE END OF THE LINE

The proud flagship was to languish in dock for the remainder of her life. She was laid up on the River Hamble, where Soper showed her off in January 1430 to a visiting Italian sea captain, the Florentine Captain of the Galleys Luca de Masa degli Albizzi, who marvelled at her construction. By 1432, she was lying in mud on the river and was struck by lightning and burnt in January 1439. By that time, she had been stripped of everything useful. It was a sad fate for a once proud ship.

The remains of the *Grace Dieu* are still visible at very low tides on the River Hamble at Bursledon bridge. She was subject to excavation by the *Time Team* archaeology programme in 2004.

1460

PREJUDICE!

MURDER

Italian merchants were important to Southampton, despite the less than hospitable feelings towards them of some of its residents. As far back as 1378, discussions were held to store Italian merchandise such as wool at Southampton Castle, which was finally being rebuilt. However, this came to nothing when the Genoese trader Janus Imperiali, sent to negotiate the deal, was murdered. London merchants were jealous of the possibility that Southampton might become the more important centre for trade.

Nevertheless, Italian trade grew, and with it, the numbers of Italians in town. In 1417, for example, a Venetian merchant called Antonio Duodo delivered £4,000 of wine in return for cloth and blankets to Southampton merchant Walter Fetplace.

Galley crews caused the same problems that port cities have had to deal with through the ages – bored sailors looking for entertainment after being cooped up on ships for weeks at a time. Fights outside the town's brothels, or over games of dice or cards were not rare.

RIOTING

By 1450 there was a thriving Italian community in Southampton, principally living in the area around Bugle Street. Not everyone wanted the Italian merchants and their families in the town, despite the prosperity their trading activities brought to the town. Anti-alien rioting in London spread to Southampton in July 1450, when a group of Romsey men came to the town to attack the Italians. They were stopped by the mayor, who had been alerted and had organised guards and patrols in the town.

In 1457, John Payne, part of a political group opposed to the Italian presence in Southampton, sued an Italian in the town and by so doing, thwarted a plan to move London Italians to Southampton. The port's reputation as welcoming to the Italian community was ruined.

PREJUDICE IN HIGH OFFICE

Things came to a head in 1460 when Payne's party formed a mob of over 100 and stormed the Guildhall, ousting the two mayoral candidates and imposing their own choice – Robert Bagswell – as mayor. By 1462 though, Payne himself was mayor and anti-alien feeling was pursued as routine. *The Black Book of Southampton* cites two examples of Payne's anti-Italian policies: two Italian merchants complained that he had seized a cargo of wine, saying that no customs payments had been made on it. The merchants provided the customs receipt, signed by Robert Belhouse, the customs collector, to prove that the accusation was untrue. However, Payne refused to return the wine and the merchants had to appeal to the High Court. Another trader, Demetri Spinelli, had been arrested for the debts of a man with a similar name, Andrew Spinelli. As Payne was one of the judges in the case, he had made sure that judgement went against Demetri.

Payne's reign came to an abrupt end in 1463 when he was removed from office by order of King Edward VI, who could see just how damaging his policies were becoming.

MUTINY

The Italian prosperity was not to last. Unrest in Italy and the growth of English shipping led to a decline in the numbers of Italian traders coming to Southampton. By 1532, the last galley fleet visited the town and is remembered for the mutiny of its crews. They attacked the captain outside the door of St Nicholas' chapel. It was a sad end to the golden Italian period in Southampton's history.

THE WARS OF THE ROSES

THE PERIOD BETWEEN 1455 and 1487 was a bitter time for Britain. The power struggle between the families of York and Lancaster, both directly descended from King Edward III (1312–1377) raged. Civil war was the order of the day and some of British history's bloodiest battles were during this time. The age of chivalry, apparent at the beginning of the wars, was put to death by cruelty as the long unrest dragged on. The Wars of the Roses exposed some of the worst atrocities human beings are capable of.

Richard Neville, Tiptoft's brother-in-law.

CRUELTY

One notable person stands out as renowned for his extreme cruelty. Unfortunately for Southampton, he visited the town in April 1470.

John Tiptoft (1427–1470) was the son of John Tiptoft, 1st Baron Tiptoft (c.1378–1443). A man of learning, he studied arts at University College Oxford and civil law at Padua University in Italy. He inherited estates in Hampshire, Middlesex and Essex. Tiptoft married Cecily, the widow of Henry Beauchamp, the Duke of Warwick (1425–1446) and the daughter of Richard Neville, the Earl of Salisbury (1400–1460) in 1449.

Cecily's aunt was the wife of Richard, Duke of York, (1411–1460) and the sister of George Neville, later Archbishop of York (c.1432–1476) and Richard Neville, Earl of Salisbury and Warwick, known as the Kingmaker (1428–1471).

In the same year, John Tiptoft was created 1st Earl of Worcester.

POLITICAL POWER

Tiptoft had wealth and was highly connected. He slowly climbed the ladder of political power. After Cecily died in 1450, he married Elizabeth Baynham, and on her death in 1452, inherited her estates in Gloucestershire. Tiptoft held appointments as Treasurer of England (1452–1454) and as joint Keeper of the Sea (1454–1457). He was also part of the king's council. Between 1458 and 1461, Tiptoft travelled and studied. He went to Venice, Jerusalem, Padua, Florence and Rome. A keen collector of books and a Latin scholar, he offered Oxford University a collection of Latin works so that students could master the style of the language.

Micklegate Bar.

MENTAL ILLNESS

Henry VI (1421–1471) was prone to mental illness. In 1453, he suffered a major mental breakdown during which he was completely unresponsive. Richard of York was appointed Lord Protector of England in March 1454 and attempted reform against Henry's favourites. Henry wanted his kingdom back in 1455 when he had recovered his sanity, but Richard had had a taste of kingship, held a legitimate claim to the throne and had determination. The seeds of civil war were sown and a series of battles were waged as each sought supremacy. After the Battle of Northampton in 1460, Henry was forced to acknowledge Richard as his heir. By the time that Tiptoft returned from his travels, Richard's son, Edward IV (1442–1483) was on the throne; Richard of York having been killed at the battle of Wakefield in 1460. It was at this point that chivalry had died – York was hacked to death on the battlefield, his seventeen year old son Edmund, the Earl of Rutland, was unceremoniously stabbed to death on a bridge by the battlefield and Richard

Neville, the Earl of Salisbury, was executed the day after the battle. All three were beheaded, their heads impaled on posts in York's Michelgate Bar and left to rot. As a lesson to the Yorkist cause, the treatment of these noblemen told all.

HIGH OFFICE

It was now time for Tiptoft to climb to high office, which he did with startling rapidity. Within two months of arriving back in England in September 1461, he was appointed to the king's council. The same month saw him take up the mantle of Chief Justice of north Wales (1461–1467) and by December he was the Constable of the Tower of London, an appointment for life. On 7 February 1462 he was Constable of England and was on a mission to try all cases of treason simply by looking at the facts of the case, without a jury being present. This he took to with a will and became known for the severity of his judgements, particularly of Lancastrian supporters. He was fond of having his victims hanged, drawn and quartered. He had the 12th Earl of Oxford, John de Vere, and his eldest son Aubrey beheaded for high treason at the Tower of London. He was created a Knight of the Garter in March 1462. More appointments followed, including that of Chancellor of Ireland, again a lifetime appointment. He accompanied Edward IV on his campaigns and was trusted in 1466 to go to Wales to capture rebels loyal to Henry VI in Harlech Castle. They had been at siege since 1461 and were to hold out against the Yorkist cause until 1468, when famine drove the famous 'Men of Harlech' (later immortalised in song) to surrender on good terms.

TORTURE

While in Ireland as deputy governor in 1467, Tiptoft had Thomas Fitzgerald, 7th Earl of Desmond and the former Deputy Governor of Ireland, and his brother-in-law Thomas Fitzgerald 7th Earl of Kildare, attainted "for alliance, fosterage, and alterage with the King's Irish enemies." He had Desmond beheaded but also had his two infant sons tortured and put to death, too. Kildare was later pardoned by the king and eventually went on to become Deputy Governor of Ireland in his own right.

REVOLTING

In 1470, Tiptoft was in Southampton with King Edward IV. The king had twenty Lancastrian prisoners, described as 'gentlemen and yeoman' by Revd J Silvester Davies in *A History of Southampton*, who had been captured after the defeat of the Duke of Clarence and the Earl of Warwick in the Lincolnshire Rebellion (the Battle of Losecote Field) in March. Clarence and Warwick had escaped to France after they had 'attempted to cut out from Southampton a large ship called *Le Trinité*' formerly belonging to Warwick. The twenty prisoners, captured at sea according to the Oxford Dictionary of National Biography on the Oxford University Press website, were given over to Tiptoft's tender care. They were found guilty of high treason and he succeeded in revolting the town's population by having them hung, drawn, quartered and impaling what remained of their bodies. They were then left for three weeks as they rotted for all to see. What the people of the town thought of Tiptoft after this, is probably not hard to guess. It is no coincidence that he became known as the 'Butcher of England,' although this nickname was circulated later.

FALL FROM GRACE

Tiptoft fell from grace when Edward IV was forced to flee to France on Henry VI's return to the throne in October 1470. He was found hiding in a tree, tried and found guilty of high treason by the 13th Earl of Oxford, John de Vere, no doubt remembering the fate of his father and brother at Tiptoft's hands. He was executed on 18 October 1470 on Tower Hill.

1563

THE PLAGUE

INFECTION

Plague was never very far away and accounts of it pop up in Southampton's history from time to time. In 1563, it 'was heavy in the town' according to Revd J Silvester Davies, who studied the history of Southampton, recorded by John Speed MD (1703–1781). In September of that year, the wife of the painter in East Street was busy painting white crosses on the doors of those households where the infection was present. By October, six men and women were employed to nurse sick people through their suffering, and then to make sure that they were carried to their graves. They were each paid 1s (5p) a week for their trouble.

VICTIMS

Between April 1583 and April 1584, in the register of deaths for the French Church, so called because the congregation were French immigrants who had permission to congregate for religious services in the chapel of God's House, the number of plague victims amongst their number is listed as seventy-one. The marriage register for 1664 also notes that the English clergy had 'abandoned their flocks' because of the plague (*A History of Southampton*).

1585

THE SPANISH ARMADA AND SOUTHAMPTON'S PIRATES

WAR!

Once again England was at war – this time with the Spanish. Privateering was the order of the day, and Southampton was central to the business and to the distribution of the booty brought back to the port. This inevitably led to the blurring of the lines between what was legal and what was considered illegal. In October 1585, arrest warrants were issued by Howard of Effingham, the Lord Admiral, for three respected Southampton merchants who, it was suspected, were dealing in pirated spoils.

The Spanish Armada.

PRIVATEERING

Privateering was a highly profitable business and it is perhaps no surprise to learn that those in prominent positions in Southampton were involved in it. In 1582, Henry Ughtred, one of Southampton's largest ship owners, was authorised by the Duke of Anjou to equip three ships to sail against the Spaniards in Peru. In 1586, the mayor, John Errington, in collaboration with John Crooke and Richard Goddard, all of whom had been trading with Spain before the war, sent the *Godspeed* out as a privateer. This ship captured the *Jacques of Dieppe*, whose cargo was owned by a Rye merchant, Nicholas Sohier. Sohier sued for the cost of the cargo and Errington and his collaborators found themselves having to pay £400 for the ship's payload.

BOOTY

Further ships were seized, prompting questions about the reach of Southampton's jurisdiction. However, these were not resolved, as enquiries were blocked by the mayor in 1587, who, it was suspected, had been one of several buyers of goods taken as prizes and sold very swiftly – before their validity as legitimate wartime booty could be established.

HOT WATER

Andrew Studley, the mayor in 1588, found himself in hot water but stood his ground when he laid claim to the ship brought in to Hamble by William Nichols. It was thought that Nichols was a pirate, and so the ship's cargo was brought to Southampton via the Itchen ferry. Howard of Effingham was displeased that the prize had not been made available to the crown and tried to claim it. He placed Studley under arrest, but the mayor would not give way. The case went to the Court of the Exchequer in 1588 and, according to Rance, the case was settled but the decision not made public. That Howard was offered a share of future sweet wine forfeitures is one indication of how the decision went.

1620

THE SEPARATISTS SAIL

RELIGIOUS INTOLERANCE

The right to worship in whatever manner one wishes has not always been a right to be enjoyed in England. The Edict of Expulsion of 1290, which King Edward I used to expel all Jews from England, is just one historical example of religious intolerance in this country.

In the seventeenth century, one group of people from the village of Scrooby in Nottinghamshire, disillusioned with what they saw as the corruption of religion in England, decided to break away from the Church of England and set up their own church. In 1606, so soon after the religious upheaval caused by Henry VIII's (1491–1547) replacement of Roman Catholicism, this stepping out of line was not viewed with favour. James I (1566–1625), smarting from the attempt on his life during the Catholic Gunpowder Plot, was determined to make sure that the new religion worked and in 1605 had introduced the unpopular Popish Recusants Act, which required Catholics to swear an oath of allegiance and to take Holy Communion in a Church of England church at least once a year.

To escape persecution, the Separatists, who called themselves 'Saints', fled to Leiden in Holland, and were able to worship as they wished. All should have been well. However, they were English people in a Dutch land. Restrictions were placed on them by Dutch craft guilds, so that they found that they were only able to obtain menial work. The population was easy-going and laid back – an attraction to the Separatists' children that was not welcome to their strict parents. No matter how hospitable their hosts were, they were not English and their new life was not working out as the Separatists had hoped. The group decided, after eleven years in exile, to leave both Holland and England behind for a new life in a new world – America.

CHRISTOPHER COLUMBUS

Christopher Columbus had stumbled across the Bahamas in 1492, so the new world was really a very young world for the Separatists. It offered a chance to start afresh, away from the secular world. It was a radical move – and one fraught with danger – but it was a move that, if it worked, would result in a life that could be lived on their terms, not on terms dictated by anyone else. The group decided to return to England on the first leg of their journey.

They were soon ready to go, having raised the finance necessary for the voyage through a London businessman. They obtained permission to settle on land on the east coast, in Virginia – named after the Virgin Queen, Elizabeth I (1533–1603). Two ships were made ready – the chartered 180-ton *Mayflower*, twelve years old and previously used for the transportation of wine, and the smaller, 60-ton *Speedwell*, originally built in Southampton and destined for use by the colony after the voyage. The *Mayflower* was made ready to sail in Southampton, while the *Speedwell* sailed to meet the *Mayflower* from Delftshaven, near Rotterdam, on 22 July 1620.

The two ships set off on their great adventure on 15 August 1620, taking with them at least one Southampton resident: John Alden, a cooper.

Christopher Columbus.

The departure of the Pilgrim Fathers.

In Southampton there are several memorials to the Pilgrim Fathers. Mayflower Park sits opposite the Mayflower Memorial, erected in 1913, on Western Esplanade. The Mayflower Theatre sits in Commercial Road. There is also a plaque, presented to the city in 1970, the 350th anniversary, by the Society of Mayflower Descendants.

TROUBLE

They hit trouble almost immediately, as the *Speedwell* sprang leak after leak. They had to put in at Dartmouth and then at Plymouth for repairs. Finally, the decision was taken to leave the *Speedwell* behind and to go on in just the one ship. 102 people, thirty-seven of them from the original Separatist group, finally sailed from Plymouth on 6 September for the perilous trip lasting sixty-six days, during which one person was lost overboard and a baby boy, Oceanus Hopkins, was born.

The ship finally arrived in Cape Cod, many miles from their target area, on 9 November 1620. They had to find a suitable place to colonise and eventually found Plymouth, named after the Plymouth Virginia Company which James I had granted a licence to colonise in 1606. They then faced a harsh winter, during which half their number perished. The Pilgrim Fathers, as the group became known, were befriended by the local indigenous population, and with their help made it to their first year in the new world. The three days of thanksgiving they celebrated on this anniversary became the Thanksgiving holiday that Americans now enjoy each year.

From Southampton, other emigrants soon followed the Pilgrim Fathers to the new world. The 150-ton *Bevis of Hampton* sailed in 1638 bound for Barbados and the 60-ton *Virgin of Hampton* left in 1640.

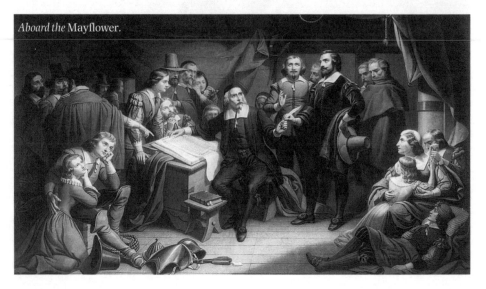

Aboard the Mayflower.

1642-1644

CAVALIERS AND ROUNDHEADS

THE DIVINE RIGHT OF KINGS

Charles I (1600–1649) believed that, because he was the king, he had the divine right to rule as he saw fit. This led to friction with Parliament, determined to see that the king stayed within the law. This difference of opinion eventually led to outright civil war. The kingdom was divided between those loyal to the king (Royalists, often known as Cavaliers), and those for the parliament (the Parliamentarians, or 'Roundheads', named after the round headgear their armies wore).

Southampton was in the Parliamentarian court at the beginning of the escalating squabble, largely because its two Members of Parliament, Edward Exton and George Gollop, were successful in converting those who were in doubt about which side was in the right. The town did, after all, have strong trading ties, which it was at pains to keep.

Charles I (Courtesy of Thomas Fisher Rare Book Library, University of Toronto)

Southampton to capture the last of the Royalist militia. They met at Hounsdown and fought for an hour, the Royalists leaderless and numbering 170. Twenty men died.

THE FIRST FIGHT

On 11 August 1642, the first battle of the Civil War occurred in Hampshire when eighty 'partisans of Parliament' (according to Tony MacLachlan's *The Civil War in Hampshire*) set out from

LEGALISED PIRACY

On 26 August the Spanish merchant ship *Santa Clara* was brought into Southampton and stripped of her cargo of silver and cochineal. In the Admiralty Register of 1644–1649, the ship is said

47

to have been taken into Southampton by Captain Bennet Strafford and the bullion 'disposed of contrary to law, without any other security given for it than the "public faith."' The Spanish Ambassador protested and the ship was eventually allowed to continue home to Spain, empty. However, the precedent had been set for legalised piracy.

PARLIAMENT ... OR ELSE!

National events were slowly gaining on Southampton. In December 1642, the town was forced to declare, once and for all, which side it was on. Captain Richard Swanley had the Parliamentarian fleet in the Solent and he sent the *Charles* into the harbour on Saturday 3 December, together with a threatening letter – the town was to declare its support for the Parliamentarian cause and submit to the Governor of Portsmouth, or face the consequences. The Revd J Davies helpfully recorded the letter and events subsequent to it in 1883 in his *A History of Southampton*:

Mr. Mayor and the rest of your Corporation,

You well know in what distractions this kingdom is in at this time. I am placed here by authority of Parliament for 'the quiet and peace of this part of the kingdom, which I shall endeavour to maintain as far as my ability of life and fortune may extend. Your town is a considerable place of merchandise, and by reason thereof are men amongst you of very good fortune and estates, and to preserve their estates, and so in general through the whole kingdom with their religion and liberty, is the only aim of the Parliament and no question those

that shall oppose either of these are unfit to enjoy either, but to be branded with baseness. There are divers reports in the country of your forwardness in opposing the Parliament herein, but I hope you wish your own peace herein better than so; if you should, there can nothing befall you but ruin and destruction. To know the truth of this I have sent my letter unto you, as likewise whether you will submit yourselves obedient to the commands of Parliament, and so consequently to the directions and commands of the Governor of Portsmouth, and the committee there authorised by both Houses of Parliament for the peace of this part of the kingdom. I have seized Calshot Castle, disabled St. Andrew's Castle and Netley Castle. I have seized all the boats of Huth [Hythe] and thereabouts. I have given orders to stop all provisions from coming out of the Isle of Wight: all which I have done by the commands of the committee at Portsmouth. I have also authority to summon you and that town to your obedience to the Grand Council of England, to which I desire an answer; if no answer, shall take it as a denial, and then if any unhappiness befall you, thank yourselves, for I shall to my uttermost endeavour use all my power to bring you thereunto. I pray you let this letter be known to the Commons as to yourselves.

Thus expecting an answer by this messenger, I rest, yours as you use yourselves,

Ri. SWANLEY.

From aboard His Majesty's ship the "Charles," the 2d of December 1642.

There is no denying that this letter must have caused consternation amongst those that read it. The desire to keep both sides happy so that trade did not suffer must have been great. Understandably though, self-preservation won through. The Mayor of Southampton sent a holding reply:

SIR, Yours of this month we received this day, about one of the clock, the contents whereof cannot be communicated to the inhabitants of this town until Monday next; in the meantime, we cannot but marvel that reports of our disaffection to the Parliament should be spread of us, not knowing that we have done any act to deserve the same. A more full answer to your letter you shall receive some time the next week.

This, with our hearty commendation to you remembered, We remain, your very loving friends,

PETER SEALE, Mayor,
Southton., 3d December 1642.

To our very loving Friend, Captain Swanley, aboard the "Charles," riding at anchor near Cowes ...

Inevitably, Southampton declared for the Parliamentarians and on the morning of 5 December 1642 sent a letter to Portsmouth a copy of which was sent to Captain Swanley.

WORTHY SIRS,
It may please you to take notice that we lately received from Captain Swanley a letter which we thought fit herewith to send you. We are heartily sorry that such suspicions should lie upon this town, being confident that there will appear no just cause for the same. Mr. Mayor has summoned the inhabitants of the 'town according to directions, and they whose names are hereunder written do cheerfully and unanimously consent and agree to submit themselves in obedience to the commands of the King and Parliament, according to the protestation by them taken, and to the directions of the committee authorised by the Parliament for the county of Southampton.

Our due respects presented, we humbly rest, your affectionate servants,

PETER SEALE, Mayor
Southton., 5th December 1642

A Parliamentary garrison then moved into Southampton and the town's defences were strengthened. The town became a strategic supply base for the Parliamentarian forces, although

Fearful of insurrection in 1643, local men were ordered to help build new defences for the town. Tony MacLachlan mentions three Stoneham men who were staked to the ground and left for hours, with a sign at their heads stating that they were 'disloyal to the common good'. Their crime? They had arrived late at the scene with their axes.

Royalist mutterings were never far beneath the surface.

Although there were battles around the town, Southampton escaped fairly lightly. Large amounts of money were demanded from the wealthier burgesses for the Parliamentarian cause, which was predictable in the circumstances. The contributions were said to be voluntary, but those who refused were deeply distrusted. The Royalists set up a garrison in Romsey in March 1644 and advanced as far as Redbridge before Parliamentarian troops stopped the move forward. They were led by Colonel Richard Norton, the Squire of Alresford, who led about 200 men. They were successful in not only surprising the Royalist troops but also managing to take captive forty prisoners, one of whom was his brother, who had chosen to side with the Royalists.

RICH PICKINGS

The town received many wounded soldiers. One batch, the Earl of Essex's troops, which had been beaten by the Royalists in Cornwall, were allowed to walk to Southampton after giving up their arms. The defeated men were then seen as rich pickings for the local folk they encountered on the long walk, and they arrived in Southampton starving, bedraggled and barefoot.

1653

THE BATTLE OF PORTLAND

THE THREE DAYS Battle, as the Battle of Portland was known, was a decisive naval engagement between the Dutch and the English that took place in February 1653 in the English Channel. The British Civil Wars website gives a good description of the whole battle, together with much background information (www.british-civil-wars.co.uk).

REGICIDE!

Relations between the two countries had been deteriorating for some time. In 1651, the Dutch turned down a proposed alliance between the English Commonwealth and the United Provinces of the Netherlands. This would have resulted in the two nations becoming a single Protestant diplomatic and trading federation. The Dutch, with a royal family of its own, were deeply suspicious of a country that could commit regicide. (King Charles I had been executed in 1649). Embarrassed that the alliance had been refused, the English drafted the Navigation Act (1651), which was aimed primarily at the Dutch but included all nationalities. The act stated that goods could be imported into the English Commonwealth territories only by English ships, or by the producing country's own ships. This was a major blow to the Dutch, who had a lucrative sea freight trade. It inevitably increased tension between the two nations and was a contributing factor to the start of the Anglo-Dutch War of 1652–54.

ENGLISH CHANNEL

By 1653 there had been several sea battles and both sides had had their victories and their losses. The Dutch, though, had won control of the English Channel at the Battle of Dungeness in November 1652 and were busy exploiting their good fortune by using the channel for trade and commerce. The English had to win the channel back if they were to stop the trade.

BATTLE COMMENCES!

Word had come that a large merchant fleet of 150 ships was returning to the Netherlands from the Mediterranean, and would be escorted through the English Channel by seventy-five Dutch naval vessels led by Lieutenant-Admiral Maarten Tromp. This was too good an opportunity to miss! Eighty English vessels assembled in three squadrons

Dutch and English ships in the midst of battle.

– Red, White and Blue – commanded jointly by Generals-at-Sea Robert Blake, George Monck and Richard Deane. The Dutch approached England on Friday 18 February, and taking advantage of the Channel's width off Portland, they attempted to slip past the English ships that had to disperse to cover the distance. Tromp drew his ships away from the merchant convoy and attacked the English, taking advantage of the favourable wind. However, by the end of the first day's fighting, his attack was broken and he was forced to regroup to cover the convoy once more. The English had lost one ship, the *Samson* with twenty-six guns, along with its commander and crew. Three ships were badly damaged; Rear-Admiral Bourne, aboard one of them, *Assistance*, was badly wounded. The Dutch lost one

commodore and twelve captains. They had one ship captured by the English and four ships destroyed. It was a bloody day's work.

Next day, hasty repairs having been made where necessary by both sides, the Dutch naval fleet had formed into a defensive formation about the rear and sides of the merchant fleet. They were off the Isle of Wight when the English ships caught up with them once more. By the night of 19 February, morale within the Dutch fleet was low. The English had succeeded in splitting off and then taking several of the merchant ships. More had taken flight, left the convoy and tried to make for French ports; the *Witte Lam* had to be taken in tow because it had lost its mast.

The 20 February was the final day of battle. The Dutch, realising that their

The doctor's bill of 1654 for looking after the prisoners amounted to a huge £106 3s 6d! (£106.17½)

only chance was to make for the French side of the Channel, where the larger English ships with deeper draughts could not follow, made a dash for it with the remains of their fleet. By this time there were only thirty-five battle-worthy Dutch naval vessels. They succeeded in squeezing past the English, and made it back to friendly waters the following day. The English, though, had proved a point. The English Channel was theirs again and the route was effectively closed to the Dutch once more. In addition, the English had captured up to fifty of the laden merchant ships, with lucrative prizes, and had taken 1,500 prisoners. The cost had been heavy though, with many wounded and up to 3,000 Dutch killed.

SOUTHAMPTON OVERWHELMED

Southampton, so close to the fighting, was a logical place for many of the prisoners to be taken. Around 1,100 of them were lodged there in March 1653, much to the consternation of the town mayor and governor. Their protests were many and varied: the town had much sickness at the time and it would be more convenient to send them elsewhere; many sick and wounded were already being cared for in private houses in the town; that when the town had garrisoned troops in 1644, more illness had broken out due to the overcrowded nature of the town. When these pleas fell on deaf ears, as noted in *A History of Southampton*, they asked that only the number of prisoners that could be accommodated in warehouses be sent, and this number should be such that only a company of sixty men would be enough to guard them (Davies, 1883).

THE PLAGUE RETURNS

THE PLAGUE RETURNED to Southampton in 1665, supposedly brought from London by a young girl sent to live with her aunt by her frightened family on 6 June. It swept through the town, causing terror, the neglect of duties many others relied on and, of course, death in large numbers.

DESPERATION

Ideas on how to protect against plague showed increasing desperation, and a fundamental lack of understanding of the causes of the disease. Wearing strong-smelling perfume or carrying a lucky charm was thought to fend off the disease, as did sniffing vinegar soaked cloths. Smoking was encouraged, even by children, as the smoke was thought also to ward off the disease. The practise of bleeding patients was also tried. This involved allowing leeches to feed off the victim's blood. It was thought that the disease would be sucked out of the unfortunate person's bloodstream. Laxatives were thought to encourage the disease to leave via the person's bowels but all this did was dehydrate victims and probably hastened their death. Drinking hot drinks was thought to enable the patient to sweat the infection out.

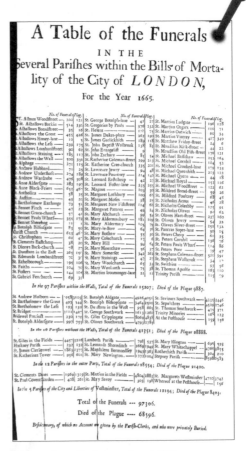

The London Bill of Mortality, 1665.

LORD HAVE MERCY

More practical was keeping the infected, and their families, away from the uninfected. Houses were closed where the infection had occurred and those within were left to live, or usually die, as God saw fit. Special measures issued by King Charles II in 1666 later made this policy compulsory. The infected person was to be removed to a special pest-house, set up specifically for the purpose, and the rest of the household were shut up inside the family home for a period of forty days. A red cross was painted on the front door, together with the words (in capitals) 'LORD HAVE MERCY UPON US'. No one was allowed to leave the property, and guards were placed to make sure that none escaped. At the end of the period, the property was opened, the dead removed or the living released, and a white cross painted on the door, which remained for a further twenty days. During this time the house was completely cleaned. None of the family's property could be taken out of the house for a further three months. The case of a desperate Isle of Wight mother in October 1665 graphically shows the results of this policy. Her daughter had been incarcerated in a Southampton house, and she hired two sailors to break her out. They did so but were caught. The unfortunate girl was put back into the house, along with one of the sailors. The other sailor, who had made it back to his ship, was later court-martialled.

7,000 DEATHS A WEEK

In London, the first recorded case was that of Rebecca Andrews on 12 April 1665 but it is probable that there were earlier cases, as those of the poor in the docks area and St Giles-in-the-Fields were not recorded. It is thought that Dutch ships, bringing cotton from Amsterdam, introduced bubonic plague.

By September 1665, 7,000 deaths a week were being recorded. It is estimated that the outbreak killed 100,000 in London alone. Many other parts of the country were infected, and Scotland closed its borders with England in an effort to keep the contagion out.

PANIC

In Southampton, the town was panic-stricken. By 26 June 1665, it was clear that the contagion had taken hold. Eight houses were closed on 27 June. There followed a steady trickle of those who could leave the town, moving as far away as possible. Pest-houses, little more than sheds, were erected outside the town to accommodate the sick.

By 5 July, the town was in trouble and calling for help from the rest of the county. Not only were people dying, but the town was not receiving provisions as deliveries were not arriving – either by reason of fear of entering an infected town, or because those providing the goods had died. Famine became a very real threat, in addition to the perils of the contagion. There was also the chance that the poor of the town, who lived in the filthy, flea-ridden backstreets that were the prime hunting grounds of the pestilence and so had a greater proportion of plague victims than other parts of Southampton, would break out of the town and then spread the contagion to a wider area. The town corporation, headed by the mayor Thomas Cornelius, sent a letter outlining the problems to the town justices in the county on 3 July and Lord Ashley, the Chancellor of the Exchequer (1621–1683), on 4 July in which they pleaded for help. They also asked Ashley if a doctor prepared to attend the sick could be sent to the town.

The reply was dated 11 July 1665, sent from Hampton Court, and gave notice that the king had decreed a fast every first Wednesday of the month throughout the period the contagion was raging, and that special collections would be made on these days. The proceeds of these collections would be made available to Southampton. In the meantime, the justices of the county were asked to help the town and a doctor was to be sent to Southampton, paid for by the king himself.

However, it was not until a further message, sent out from Southampton to the justices on 15 July, which told of the 'sad and lamentable' condition of the town that any material help arrived from the county. By that time, the Corporation needed £150 a week to keep going and was in dire distress. The usual sources of funding, including those residents who gave to the less fortunate, had virtually dried up as people died or were reduced to needing charity themselves. It is easy to forget that there were only six weeks between 6 June and 15 July, and plague was in many other parts of the country, too. In those few weeks, the town had been reduced from a busy and reasonably prosperous port to having to beg for help from just about anybody who might be

able to do so. Funds began to pour into Southampton from towns and cities, the great and the good. From a long list of donations listed in *A History of Southampton*, some stand out. Thomas Wriothesley, 4th Earl of Southampton (1607–1667) sent £50, as did the town of Dorchester. Portsmouth gave £57, the parish of Titchfield £28 and Poole £28 6s 7d (£28.33). Marlborough sent £46, Lymington £36.8s (£36.40) and the villages of Netley, Bitterne, Botley, Bursledon and Hamble combined contributed £18 15s 11d (£18. 80). A grand figure of £50 came from the king from the first day of the monthly fast, and the town of Sarum sent £70. The king's court was at Sarum at the time, and a further £41 came from the Close at Sarum, no doubt boosted by donations from courtiers. The king also gave twenty tuns of French wine (a tun being 252 gallons in a cask), half a tun of which the Corporation was able to distribute amongst the poor. They were able to sell the rest on, bringing in a further £242.15s (£242.75).

DESERTERS

In the meantime, those who had deserted their posts were being brought to book. John Steptoe, mayor in 1664 and deputy mayor at the time of the plague, was

Black rats carried the plague. As the disease killed the rats, the fleas they hosted migrated to new hosts: humans. One of the preventive measures taken was to eradicate dogs and cats. These were natural rat predators, and so the rat population was allowed to explode, making the plague contagion that much worse.

the most prominent of the deserters. He was fined £20 for 'neglecting to give his assistance in this time of affliction'. Deserters ranged from churchwardens, collectors for the poor and the town steward to the chief bailiff and the water-bailiff. It is easy to see how Southampton struggled to cope when people died in large numbers, but it became almost impossible when officials whose job it was to run the town left their posts to save themselves. In the circumstances, it is easy to understand the desire for self-preservation, but the hardship caused is not so easy to dismiss.

The plague diminished slightly over the summer, increased in September and dipped again in December. By August 1666, the death toll had decreased to two in the preceding month.

1773

GEORGIAN SOUTHAMPTON
Polygon

A GRAND IDEA

Southampton had a short period as a spa and resort town in the Georgian period (1714–1830). The Prince of Wales came to Southampton to bathe in the sea, and the waters of one particular stream were thought to be of medicinal benefit. Hotels were built to cater for the influx of visitors, and the town's population doubled. Attempts were made to bring an upmarket garden suburb to the outskirts of the town, but street lighting and paving lagged behind the construction.

In 1768, Polygon was conceived. Its aim was to offer a more upmarket residential and social area of the town, situated to the north of the town walls. It was to cater for the needs of the nobility and gentry who both lived in the town and who visited it, but it was never fully completed, as one of the designers went bankrupt after building only three houses and the hotel.

The central building was a fine hotel, which Mrs James Harris described in 1771 as having a ballroom, card room, tearoom and two billiard rooms. There were also restaurants, fifty bedrooms and stabling for 500 horses.

TOSSED LIKE A FOOTBALL

Lack of street lighting beyond Above Bar led to Polygon becoming a dangerous place to travel, as visitors were sometimes robbed or assaulted. The *Hampshire Chronicle* of September 1773 gives an account of a gentleman who should have taken a sedan chair or travelled in a carriage. Dressed as a shepherd for a masked ball, the 'mob insulted him greatly by throwing him down and tossing him like a football'. 'Some humane persons' passing by eventually rescued him. This ball was also marred by the throwing of a large stone through the window, which nearly hit the Duke and Duchess of Gloucester.

Eventually, Polygon's situation (a mile out of town) let it down and custom declined. The elegant hotel became residences and the area was added to in piecemeal fashion. It had become a place for respectable families by the 1830s.

1786

A PEACEFUL SPA TOWN?

BY THE EIGHTEENTH century, the town was no longer on the alert for invading or marauding Frenchmen. The port was peaceful and fashionable as a spa town, since the discovery of a Chalybeate spring in 1740. Royalty and other notables came to Southampton to take the waters, and it became rich as a consequence.

There was, though, a need for a prison. In 1774, the cost of making God's House Tower into the town gaol was £140. Of this, the Pavement Commissioners for Southampton paid £100 and the county provided the rest. The tower, which was already being used as a house of correction (Bridewell), became the town gaol in 1786. It was in use as a prison until 1855.

God's House Tower was the site of the 1876 statue of Prince Albert, by William Theed, which was presented to the town by five-times mayor Sir Frederick Perkins. He paid £300 for the figure. The statue was sculpted in terracotta and deteriorated quickly. It was taken away for storage in 1907, when it was thought its condition would cause offense to Prince Albert's grandson, Kaiser William II, on his visit to Southampton. The statue was later destroyed.

After the prison closed, God's House Tower faced twenty years of idleness until the tower became a store. It remained in this lowly function until 1957, when plans were made to turn it into a museum. In 1961, it opened its doors to the public as the Museum of Archaeology. The building of the SeaCity museum made the God's House Tower site redundant and it closed in 2011.

1848 & 1865

CHOLERA STRIKES SOUTHAMPTON

SEXY SEWERS?

It seems a strange thing to say, but when reading a history of Southampton it becomes apparent that when the town was evolving during the Victorian age, more attention seems to have been paid to the provision of its parks than to its drainage. The simple fact seemed to be that parks were seen as 'sexy'; sewers were not.

In 1844, the City Corporation obtained an Act of Parliament, the Marsh Act, to enclose common land to make it into public parks, for recreation and health purposes. There had been critics of the policy, as it was feared that the land would be built upon and thus lost as green spaces in the growing town. The fact is, however, that opposing sides at the corporation worked together to enshrine the parks; and it is to this act that we owe the green parks we have today.

EPIDEMICS

If only the same unifying force had been used with regard to public sanitation. If it had, the cholera epidemics of 1848–49, which killed 240 people, and of 1865, which saw more residents dead, would probably not have occurred.

DEATH

Cholera symptoms include quick-onset watery diarrhoea, which resembles the milky colour of water used to rinse rice; nausea and vomiting that can go on for several hours; rampant dehydration; muscle cramps and shock. This nasty disease can result in a coma and then death, and frequently did. Even those who have been exposed to cholera but show no symptoms are capable of passing it on to other people in their stools for up to two weeks after infection.

Contaminated water supplies are the main cause of Cholera, although eating infected raw shellfish and uncooked vegetables and fruit can also cause it.

ALARM!

It would be wrong to say that no one was interested in the fact that there was cholera in Southampton. There was, in fact, widespread alarm that it had occurred. A committee was formed to look into the matter at the first outbreak, and it looked into conditions where the victims were living – the slums. Tim Lambert, in his excellent localhistories. org website, tells us that of 230 streets in 1840s Southampton, 145 were without sewers and it was common for up to seventy-seven people to share one toilet. Only main streets were paved and cleaned; the rest were ignored. However, it was within these filthy backstreets that disease festered. The committee noted 'manure heaps, pigsties, piles of entrails of fish and other animal matter and broken drains.' They also noted that waste from the Royal Hotel at Houndwell drained into the ground surrounding it. It was not unusual for conditions like this to be prevalent in a town at the time. The residents who were most likely to be living there were poor and ill-educated. They therefore had little influence and their living conditions could safely be ignored, as they were in other towns. However, disease could be spread, and that would never do. The committee issued handbills telling the population what to do in an epidemic, but this was not enough to save the lives of the 240 residents cholera killed that summer.

STRIFE

Political squabbling soon began between those who thought that something should be done to eradicate the conditions in which the disease could flourish, using the new Public Health Act, and local Conservatives, anxious that the imposition of a Southampton Local Board of Health that would levy taxes to do its work would result in property prices dropping. The Borough Council sided with the Conservatives and sent a notice to the Public Health Board stating that the existing arrangements in the town were satisfactory and a Local Board of Health was not needed. However, the Public Board of Health appointed a Southampton inspector, William Ranger in 1849, no doubt influenced by a petition sent by the P&O Port Superintendent, Captain Engledue, appalled by the living conditions the P&O employees and their families lived in. Ranger's subsequent report listed many causes for concern, including overflowing middens, un-emptied toilets and a pond filled with the decaying

SOUTHAMPTON'S FIRST DRINKING FOUNTAIN

In an age when piped water was still unavailable, water fountains were popular. They provided a non-alcoholic option for working people and helped in the fight against cholera. They also often provided troughs for animals to drink from, an important consideration in an age before motorised transport.

The first of Southampton's drinking fountains was installed at the insistence of Edmund Kell, a clergyman, who moved to the town in 1853 after many years on the Isle of Wight. Shocked that working men only seemed to have alcohol to drink when not at home, he attracted the attention of Charles Melly, a wealthy Liverpudlian with experience of installing drinking fountains in his hometown. Melly paid for a drinking fountain, which was erected in 1859, on the corner of Marsh Lane, East Street and St Mary Street. The Grade II listed obelisk can now be seen in Hound Park, where it was relocated in 1969.

corpses of animals and unwanted babies. It was not surprising that a public health order was issued for Southampton in 1849. The pond in question, at Padwell Cross, was filled in and a water trough (later a drinking fountain) was put in its place.

MONEY

This was not the magic wand the town had hoped for, however. The town's poor were still enduring the same squalid conditions over fifteen years later, when, in 1865, cholera broke out again. Something had to be done. James Lemon, engineer, was appointed to sort out the drainage in Southampton, but he had his work cut out to get it done. As with most things, the root cause of all the objections was money and the effect that paying for the engineering work necessary to bring proper sanitation to the town would have. It took until 1875 to come up with a comprehensive plan for all parts of the town to be properly drained. Even then, it took a petition in 1871 from the people of Oxford Street and a compulsory purchase of land at St Denys for a sewage works to get things on their way to the plan. Portswood, whose councillor had ridiculed the idea of sewers, eventually had a three-section drainage system installed, ensuring that the whole area was covered.

Conditions slowly improved, and the opening of a new waterworks at Otterbourne in 1888 hastened matters, as by then most people had piped water and no longer relied on wells, ponds or pumps for their supply.

1855

MURDER, MOST HORRID!

THE COUNTRY AGOG

Southampton, no less than any other sizable town in Britain, has had its fair share of crime. In 1855 the whole country was agog at the murder of Naomi Kingswell, upper housemaid to the Revd and Mrs Poynder and their three children at 1 Moira Place, Upper Above Bar Street on Sunday 14 October 1855. Newspapers across the land reported the gory details.

The London Standard of 16 October and *The Lancaster Gazette* of 20 October 1855 give Naomi's age as twenty-six years. *The London Standard,* which devoted over 2,000 words to the 'Horrible Murder at Southampton,' further states that she was of 'respectable family, and very prepossessing appearance.' She had met Abraham Baker when they both lived in Ryde, on the Isle of Wight. When he moved to Southampton in July 1855, to take up the position of footman at the Poynder household, she followed a month later, as he was able to secure her the housemaid's job.

BLOOD FLOWS

All seemed to be well for a few months, but things changed. On the fateful day, Naomi and the cook, Charlotte Lacey, were in the kitchen when there was a knock on the door. Naomi answered it and let Baker in. He was quiet and told the cook, on her enquiry, that he had not been to church that day. She asked him to lay lunch out for her, which he did, going into the pantry to load trays and walking between the two areas several times. He then came back into the kitchen, produced a duelling pistol and shot Naomi in the head at close range. Charlotte testified at the committal proceedings that Naomi's final word was, 'Oh!' as she slid to the floor, blood flowing freely. She further stated that the gun was the width of a finger away from Naomi's head when the trigger was pulled.

Charlotte called for assistance and Police Constable George Thatchell took Baker into custody. Charlotte said, 'Baker, Baker, what have you done?' To this he replied, 'I have done it. She deserved it.'

The police retrieved the gun from the pantry where Baker had stashed it. At the committal proceedings, High Street Southampton gun maker Alfred Clayton testified that Baker had bought the gun from him the day before the murder. Baker had gone to him to buy a double-barrelled gun, but had settled for a single-barrelled dueling pistol because it was cheaper. With bullets, powder and caps

At Abraham Baker's committal proceedings, the police officer attending the scene, 'Serjeant Ralfs,' as reported by the *London Standard*, caused a sensation when he told the court that the half-inch ball, which had been shot through the victim's head at point blank range, had 'struck the ceiling and the wall and from thence glanced over the door of the kitchen … I found the ball in the hairs of a long-handled brush … I found some small piece of the skull which had been forced across the room, and were lying near where the ball was found.'

the cost was 15s 6d (77 ½p). Baker had told the gun maker that he wanted the gun to shoot a 'large dog'.

THE LETTER

At the proceedings it emerged that Baker had written a letter to his family in Newport, Isle of Wight, on the morning of 14 October. In it he said that it would be the last letter they received from him. He gave instructions about the disposal of his possessions and where to find them. Several personal articles were gifted to them in the letter. This letter had been retrieved from the Post Office, opened at the police station and read out in court. The clear implication was that the police thought he had been preparing to commit suicide after the murder.

COMMITTAL PROCEEDINGS

The committal proceedings were on Monday 15 October 1855 at the Audit House, in front of presiding magistrate mayor Sampson Payne and five others on the bench, including the former mayor J. T. Tucker. Abraham Baker is described by *The London Standard* as being of a 'delicate' appearance and having the look of a 'mechanic'. He was calm throughout, but broke down when he saw and spoke to his father. He had no questions for any of the witnesses. He was sent for trial at Winchester on a charge of murder.

At the trial, he was found guilty and then made a full confession. He had killed Naomi because he had been driven wild with jealousy. His marriage proposal had been rejected. A new wedding ring was found in his possession at the time of his arrest. Abraham Baker was hanged at Winchester Gaol on 8 January 1856.

Naomi Kingswell was buried in an unmarked pauper's grave in Southampton Old Cemetery.

This song first appeared as a broadside ballad soon after the trial. Broadsides were produced and sold on the streets as single sheets in the eighteenth and nineteenth centuries, as a means of spreading news. They were written in the form of verse, and as a result many of them have found their way into the folk song repertoire. This was published by Milestones publishing and performed by Brian Hooper and Jeff Henry. The writer is unknown.

Southampton Tragedy
Reproduced from John Paddy Brown's *Folk Songs of Old Hampshire*.
Arranged by Brian Hooper and Jeff Henry

Within a jail I am lamenting, will no one shed a tear for me,
In agony I'm sore relenting, the author of a tragedy,
I dearly loved Naomi Kingswell, but she alas proved false to me,
I in Southampton did her murder, at the age of twenty three.

Oh my sad name is Abraham Baker, I gazed on Naomi with delight,
And we were both reared up so tender, in Newport in the Isle of Wight,
And pleasant hours we passed together in sweet love and harmony,
So fondly I did love my Naomi, and I thought she loved me.

In Southampton we fellow servants lived; oh, how dreadful is my case,
All with the Rev Mr Poynder, at number One in Moira Place,
My mind was always agitated unless I could my Naomi see,
And oh so fondly I did love her, but Naomi did look cold on me.

I did prepare a fatal pistol, and on the blessed Sabbath day,
Determined I went to the kitchen, my own true love to kill and slay,
So suddenly I drew that trigger, in her poor head I placed that ball,
And I did slay my own Naomi, she on the kitchen floor did fall.

Oh my father, oh my mother, can you view the deed I've done,
And shed one single tear of sorrow for your sad unhappy son,
Who at the Bar must shortly answer, for that sad and dreadful deed,
You Southampton men and maidens my confession closely read.

In the dark cells of Southampton, a wretch I lie both day and night,
In the midst of youth, in the midst of vigour, scarcely reached the prime of life,
The deed I did now makes me shudder, my guilty heart it wounds with pain,
Oh God, receive me in your mansion to dwell with Naomi once again.

'DR LIVINGSTONE, I PRESUME ...'

COFFIN

Dr David Livingstone has a slight connection to Southampton. Sadly, it was not for good works within the city or for having family in the area. As A. G. K. Leonard points out (*More Stories of Southampton's Streets*), Southampton's claim to Livingstone fame is that the coffin bearing the great explorer's body was landed at the Royal Pier on 15 April 1874, on its way to interment in Westminster Abbey.

David Livingstone had spent his life working in Africa as a medical doctor, missionary and explorer. He was born in Scotland in 1813 to working-class parents living in one room of a tenement owned by the mill he was eventually to work in from the age of ten. His father taught him to read and write and he taught himself Latin. By 1836 he had earned enough money to begin studying medicine at Anderson's University, Glasgow. After taking a

The coffin bearing the great explorer Dr Livingstone's body was landed at the Royal Pier on 15 April 1874, on its way to interment in Westminster Abbey. Flags were flown at half mast in the town.

Dr Livingstone.

break in his studies to spend time at the London Missionary Society, he returned to medicine to finish his studies. In 1840, the Society ordained him as a missionary. He wanted to go to China, but civil unrest there prevented it and in December he sailed instead to Africa as a missionary doctor.

TROPICAL DISEASES

Livingstone spent thirty-two years there, until his death in 1873; first bringing the 'civilising' benefit of western religion to the 'savages' and then exploring the continent. He was particularly interested in discovering the source of the Nile. He met and married his wife Mary Moffat in Kuraman, where she was teaching, in 1845. He was a prolific writer and a keen observer, particularly of tropical diseases. He was often the first person from Europe to meet local people and he gained their trust as a healer, often being in such

demand that he had to limit the services he offered. His realised that quinine was effective against malaria and his recipe for pills to be taken as a remedy (he called them 'Livingstone's Rousers' for the rousing effect they had on the patient) was still being used in the 1920s. He also made the connection between malaria and mosquitoes many years before the link was officially proved.

ORDEAL

Henry Morton Stanley (born John Rowlands in 1841), a journalist for the *New York Herald* and one-time adventurer, was sent to find Livingstone, who had penetrated so deeply into the African interior that no news of him had been heard of for some six years. The trip was an ordeal, as disease took its toll on Stanley's retinue during the 700-mile journey from Zanzibar to Ujiji near Lake Tanganyika, in what is now known as Tanzania, where he finally found his quarry. He may then have uttered the famous words, 'Dr Livingstone, I presume.'

Henry Morton Stanley in his train.

Dr Livingstone meets Mr Stanley.

Certainly, news of the meeting and subsequent four months of travels with him were published in the *Herald* and also in the *New York Times*. Stanley subsequently wrote a book about his travels, *How I Found Livingstone; Travels, Adventures, and Discoveries in Central Africa* (1871). All of this attention brought Livingstone's name and work to an interested public.

Livingstone had failing health, but refused to return to England and died in Chief Chitambo's village at Ilala, near the Bangweulu Swamps in Zambia. His attendants recorded the date of his death as 4 May 1873, which is the date given on his death certificate and on his African memorial, although 1 May 1873 may have been the date he actually died. His heart was buried under a tree in the village, as the local people said that his heart belonged to Africa. A

memorial was also set up there, which was replaced by the current Livingstone Memorial in 1902.

Livingstone's body, embalmed in a cylinder of bark, was shipped back to England for burial in Westminster Abbey. When the coffin arrived in Southampton on board the P&O ship Malwa, town mayor Edwin Jones, who had arranged for the ship to land its precious cargo at the port, orchestrated civic ceremonies to honour the great man on his return to England.

Amongst his reception committee were Livingstone's father in law Dr Robert Moffatt and the reporter H. M. Stanley. Flags flew at half mast in the town and a procession progressed through High Street, Bernard Street and Oxford Street, lined with thousands of mourners, to take his body from the pier to Terminus Station. It was loaded on to a train to take it to the Royal Geographical Society headquarters at No. 1 Saville Row in London to lie in state, while awaiting burial in the centre of the nave in Westminster Abbey. His funeral on 18 April 1874 was attended by his four surviving children; his faithful African servant Jacob Wainwright who had escorted the body from Africa and who had to be restrained from throwing himself into the grave with Livingstone's coffin; many members of the missionary and learned communities and the general public.

The Mayor of Southampton and the town's Reception Committee attended the funeral as guests of the Royal Geographical Society.

1884

SHIPWRECKED!

DRAWING STRAWS

In the days before unions and health and safety laws, when the owner of a ship was the master of all he surveyed and whose word was law for his workforce, it was not uncommon for ships to be sacrificed for their insurance value. It was also a useful way to avoid paying wages to expensive sailors. Some ships were not maintained for this very reason, and the result of this was that there were often shipwrecks. Sailors who found themselves *in extremis* due to being shipwrecked were often in a no-win situation, forced to make decisions that in normal circumstances would have repulsed them. Cannibalism was informally acknowledged as the only thing to do when there was no other way out of a situation, and all sailors understood what the term 'drawing straws' meant.

RICHARD PARKER

The story of the unfortunate Richard Parker is well known in Southampton. He was a seventeen-year-old orphan in 1854 when he signed on as an ordinary seaman at the rate of £1 15s (£1.75) a month. Born in Itchen Ferry Village, Richard was looking for excitement. He joined the crew of the rickety 33-ton yacht *Mignonette*, owned by a wealthy lawyer from Australia, John Henry Want. The yacht had spent the winter sitting in mud in Tollesbury, Essex, and this experience was not good for its timbers. Thomas Dudley, the master of the vessel, and the crew were to sail the ship to Australia for its owner.

The ship sailed first to Southampton, encountering a storm on the way, which laid bare the problems a winter sitting in mud had caused. The ship was repaired at the J. G. Fay & Co. shipyard on what is now Shamrock Quay. All three crewmen left the vessel, leaving Dudley to find a new crew who would not be put off by the yacht's condition.

Dudley recruited two others besides young Richard. Local Sotonian Edwin Stephens was next to sign on, as mate. Edward Brooks, who became the yacht's able seaman, soon followed him. Both these men were in their late thirties and married with children. The crew now complete, the *Mignonette* sailed on the first leg of her long journey, leaving Southampton on 19 May 1884.

All was well and the voyage continued until the ship reached Madeira on 1 June 1884. Here Richard took the opportunity to send a letter to his foster parents, Captain Jack and Mrs Mathews in Itchen

Ferry Village. In it, he said that he was happy, having had a good voyage.

IN TROUBLE

Twelve hours later, the newly provisioned vessel left for the next leg of their long voyage. The *Bride of Lorne* sighted them two weeks later. This was the last time the *Mignonette* was seen. By the end of June, after they had crossed the equator, they were in trouble. Gathering storms brought high winds and the *Mignonette* protested. By 3 July, the waves pounding on the weak hull had resulted in an unstoppable leak. The angry sea breached the stricken craft on 5 July and it was the end. They were 1,600 miles (2,600km) north-west of the Cape of Good Hope. Tom Dudley gave the order to abandon ship and the vessel's 13ft dinghy was hastily launched. Richard was ordered to throw a barrel of fresh water overboard, in the hope that it would float and they would be able to pick it up later. Dudley, the captain, was the last to leave, going below to try to grab as much food as possible, along with a compass and sextant. He nearly went down with his ship, as it was only the urgent shouting of his crew that alerted him to the fact that the yacht was about to sink beneath the raging waves. He scrambled out as the vessel sank around him. In the process, he dropped all but two of the cans of food he had grabbed. When he was hauled onto the bobbing dinghy, it was found that he had rescued tins of turnip.

NIGHTMARE

This was the start of a nightmare that must have seemed never-ending to the four participants. Unlike modern lifeboats, equipped with provisions and shelter, the crew of the *Mignonette* were lucky they had their oilskins on, as these were their shelter on the tiny dinghy that they found themselves crammed into. The barrel of water, so carefully saved from the stricken craft, had been flung out of sight by the ferocious storm and the meagre food ran out very quickly. They rigged a sail as best they could and thanked the stars that they had a compass and sextant. They were hundreds of miles off the coast of Trinidad.

A passing turtle's bad luck was the crew's good fortune, as the animal's meat kept them alive for the next two weeks. By then, they were drinking their own urine.

On 20 July Richard foolishly drank seawater to try to slake his fiery thirst. He was to pay heavily for so rash an act, as his body reacted to the salty liquid. He gradually slipped into semi-consciousness and delirium.

Captain Tom Dudley, wearied as they all were by lack of food and water and the swings in temperature from boiling during the day to freezing at night, now began to speak of drawing straws. This referred to the unacknowledged practice of lots being drawn amongst those present, with the loser being sacrificed to feed the rest. Needless to say, this was not a popular subject. Dudley persisted, pointing to the boy lying on the floor of the dinghy, gasping for breath. By his own admission, he argued that the one near to death, and who had no dependents, would be the logical person to sacrifice. Brooks would have no part in it. Stephens argued for more time for rain or to sight a ship. By daybreak the next day, 25 July, neither had been seen and so Stephens

Edgar Allen Poe wrote the unsuccessful novel *The Narrative of Arthur Gordon Pym of Nantucket*, some forty years before the tragic events following the sinking of the *Mignonette*. In the story, the crew of a ship are wrecked and, after days of starvation adrift on the high seas, straws are drawn for one of the crew to be sacrificed for food so that the others could survive. The cabin boy drew the short straw. His name was ... Richard Parker.

agreed with Dudley that Richard should be 'put out of his misery'. Dudley acted swiftly. He put a penknife into Richard's throat and the lad died instantly.

The unfortunate teenager's body was to feed all three for four days, his heart and liver being eaten while they were still warm. When a ship was finally sighted, on 29 July, and they were safely aboard the German ship *Moctezuma*, Dudley had no hesitation in giving an honest version of the events leading up to their rescue. He felt secure in the knowledge that what he had done was for the survival of the majority and this would be accepted, it being a Custom of the Sea. What was left of poor Richard was tossed into the watery depths by one of the German sailors.

Unfortunately for Dudley, this was not the way it was seen by the authorities when they returned to England. For the first time in centuries, the Law of the Land challenged the Law of the Sea. All three survivors found themselves arrested in Falmouth, where they had been landed, and charged with the murder of Richard Parker. They were amazed! Had not the circumstances been such that the death of the weakest, the one that was dying anyway and had no wife or family depending on him, been justified for the benefit of the rest?

READ ALL ABOUT IT!

Media interest in the case was intense, with newspapers as far apart as the *North Devon Journal* and the *Glasgow Herald* reporting each history-making step in the proceedings. The *Sheffield and Rotherham Independent* covered the story in great depth on 13 December 1884, when it was able to bring the verdict, sentence and subsequent decision on the sentence to its readers.

The three were first brought up in front of local Falmouth magistrates on 8 September, when they expected to be dismissed and allowed to go home to their families. Instead, they were remanded in custody while advice was sought from the Treasury Solicitor in London, a new requirement of all magistrates on murder cases. The facts of the case went through the ranks of the civil service and ended with the Home Secretary, Sir William Harcourt, who took the decision to prosecute the three. Similar cases had come before the courts and had ended in acquittal on legal technicalities; the government was determined to try to put an end to the Custom of the Sea if it could.

The case against Brooks, the one crewmember who had not taken part in Richard's death, was dropped and he was then called as a prosecution

The Nuffield Youth Theatre, with Fairbridge, Solent and Great Oaks Schools, recreated the story of the fate of Richard Parker in their play, *Mr Parker's Bones*, subtitled *or The Strange, Lamentable, Bloody and mostly true History of Parker of Peartree Green and of his Captain, the dastardly Cannibal Tom*. Inviting their audience to the 'trial of the century', the two performances were held in Court 1 of Southampton's old Magistrates Court at the Civic Centre in January 2009.

witness. The case was then referred to the Cornwall and Devon winter Assizes.

SENSATIONAL FACTS

Baron Huddleston (1815–1890), a judge with a reputation for directing juries, heard the case. Was necessity a defence against murder? Much of the population, having heard the sensational facts and subsequently having got up a collection for the men's defence, thought it was. The Home Secretary thought otherwise, hence Huddleston's selection as the presiding judge.

Dudley and Stephens pleaded not guilty. However, no testimony for the defence was allowed and Brooks gave full evidence of the actions of the other two on the fateful day. It was only under cross-examination that the full extent of the situation faced by the crew became apparent to the court. This questioning also brought to light Brooks' own cannibalism.

In the end, Huddleston gave the jury two options. They could accept his direction to find the men guilty of murder or they could return a special verdict, a verdict last brought in 1785 and an option almost forgotten, which allowed the jury to state the facts and the judge to decide the verdict. Either way, what

the judge had clearly already decided to be the verdict would be the one brought down on the heads of the accused. Huddleston did not wait for the jury to reach a decision, instead bringing in the special verdict himself, which he had written the night before. What followed was a shambles, as Huddleston later changed parts of the pre-written special verdict to ensure that it held no mistakes that could trip up the case later on.

Eventually, on 4 December, after much legal wrangling about the rights or otherwise of the Huddleston hearing, the case came before Lord Chief Justice Lord Coleridge, the head of a panel of three judges, in London. Despite the best efforts of Arthur J. H. Collins, QC, for their defence, the verdict of murder was given. Necessity was not held to be a defence against murder. The two men were sentenced to death, with a recommendation to mercy. However, it was not until 12 December that they heard that the sentence had been commuted to six months hard labour. The *Sheffield and Rotherham Independent* of 13 December reported the men to be 'in capital spirits' by the news.

Cabin boy Richard Parker was only seventeen years of age when he met an unfortunate end when shipwrecked in 1884. He is remembered in the cemetery at Peartree Church.

MEMORIAL

Richard's family still reside in Southampton. Recently, a marble slab laid horizontally in the yard replaced his old headstone memorial, which had decayed over the years. It rests in the little churchyard at Pear Tree Church, the oldest Anglican Church in the world, having been built in 1618 and consecrated in 1620. The giant gleaming stone explains the circumstances of Richard's death.

1896

MURDER IN PORTSWOOD

FAITHFUL?

Thirty-eight-year-old Angelina Faithfull may well not have lived up to her name, but that was no reason to take her life.

She was living with a Southampton dock labourer, twenty-four-year-old Frederick Burden in Brooklyn Road, Portswood in 1896. It was known that other men visited her from time to time and this was why, so the prosecution said, Burden snapped and in a fit of jealous rage, cut his common-law wife's throat.

Burden protested his innocence when he was arrested, saying that at the time of the murder (7 April, a Thursday morning at 9 o'clock), he was more than ten miles away in Winchester, near the barracks there.

BLOOD STAINS

However, his clothing – covered in blood – told another tale. He explained that the blood was his own, as he had fallen into barbed wire. It took two trials at the Hampshire Assizes to get a conviction though. At the first, the jury failed to agree and the case crumpled. Did Burden kill his wife? Or did one of the many men who visited her do so?

Frederick Burden has the distinction of being part of the last triple execution in the country.

Eighteen-year-old Private Samuel Smith of the 4th King's Royal Rifles stationed at Farnborough Barracks, who shot dead Corporal Robert Payne for putting him on a disciplinary charge, was another of the party.

The pair were joined by thirty-two year-old Phillip Matthews, a Teignmouth Council coachman, who bigamously married his third wife, fifteen-year-old Charlotte Malhoney, whereupon his second wife left him and their six-year-old daughter Elsie. A small child being an encumbrance when married to a fifteen-year-old, Matthews strangled the little girl and left her in a wood.

The three murderers were hanged at Winchester Gaol on Tuesday 21 July 1896. After this execution, the condemned were put to death singly as it was deemed cruel to have prisoners waiting for long periods on the gallows with nooses around their necks while the other prisoners were made ready to join them.

1899

MARY ANN ROGERS
AND THE *STELLA*

AT THE TIME, the disaster that overwhelmed the *Stella*, a passenger steamer belonging to the London and South West Railway, was a major event, only eclipsed by the *Titanic* catastrophe in 1912.

Two railway companies ran services to the Channel Islands; the London and South West from Waterloo via Southampton, and the Great Western from Paddington via Weymouth. This was great in theory, as there was a choice of service for passengers to choose from, but the ports of St Peter Port in Guernsey and St Helier in Jersey were each only big enough to take one of the ships at the time. This was inconvenient, to say the least, and led, ultimately, to great loss of life.

On Thursday 30 March 1899, Maundy Thursday, both companies ran a special Easter excursion to St Peter Port that was scheduled to arrive at the same time – 5.30 in the afternoon. It was left to the ship's captains to ensure that they got their ship into port first. This folly led to the two ships racing each other to be the winner and so able to claim the berth.

On that morning 147 passengers joined the *Stella* and her crew at number four berth, Eastern Docks. The ship left Southampton at 11.25 in the morning, already ten minutes later than scheduled. The fair weather soon changed once the open sea was gained, and banks of fog meant that the ship had to keep slowing down. In between each bank, the ship ran at full speed until just before the ship neared the notorious Casquets rocks, when it continued at full speed even though the fog had once again descended.

The *Stella's* Captain, Captain Reeks, the second mate and the chief mate all congregated on the bridge and listened for the Casquets' lighthouse foghorn, which would tell them how near they were to the rocks. Just before 4 o'clock, the horn sounded, very close. Too close, in fact, for the ship's crew to react in time to stop them from hitting the jagged edges in the water. The ship ploughed into the rocks, despite the Captain ordering 'full speed astern' and trying to manoeuvre away from the danger. At the speed the ship was going – 18 knots – there was little time to spare. Both sides of the ship were scored and she ran straight through Black Rock, eight miles west of Alderney, which ripped her hull. She was doomed.

The *Stella* took just eight minutes to sink. During that time, it was reported that there was no panic. Women and children were helped into the

There is a canopied drinking fountain memorial to Mary Ann Rogers opposite the Mayflower Park on the Western Esplanade. Erected by public subscription, it was unveiled in 1901.

In 1899, the sinking of the passenger steamer Stella, *whilst on its way to the Channel Islands, shocked Southampton. Mary Ann Rogers' heroic self-sacrifice enabled others to survive the ship's demise. A memorial is dedicated to her and the* Stella.

lifeboats first, and most of these were successfully lowered from the stricken craft. All aboard had life vests, but there were not enough lifeboats for the passengers and crew on board. One of the collapsible lifeboats only partially opened and sank when it was in the water, and one of the wooden boats capsized, although wave action later righted it, allowing some of the fourteen clinging to it to get aboard. Several passengers were drowned as the boat was swung over and more died later of exposure from being in the cold water. The French naval vessel *Marsouin* finally picked up only eight survivors from this lifeboat, twenty-seven hours later.

Those aboard the lifeboats watched as the *Stella*, with her captain, most of her crew and many passengers still aboard, slipped beneath the waves.

One person who lost her life that day was Mrs Mary Ann Rogers, a stewardess who had worked for the company since her husband had drowned whilst also working for the London and South West Railway in 1883. During those last minutes, she worked tirelessly to make sure that women and children had lifebelts, and even gave up her own to a child. She refused to take a place in a lifeboat for fear of capsizing it, and was last seen waving goodbye while calling to those in the lifeboat she had refused a place in to be of 'good cheer' (www. jakesimpkin.org).

The survivors were eventually picked up, two boats by the London and South West Region steamer *Vera* which landed in Jersey and the other two by the Great Western steamer *Lynx*, en-route to Guernsey.

111 people lost their lives on the *Stella*.

15 APRIL 1912

A TITANIC DISASTER

THE PRIDE OF THE FLEET

The White Star Line was proud of its fleet of state-of-the-art luxury cruise vessels, the *Olympic* class liners. They were larger than any other ship in operation on the seas at the time. The *Olympic* and the *Titanic* were the first built of three planned. The *Gigantic* (later renamed the *Britannic*) was to follow.

They were the pride of the shipping line and were meant to allow the company to sail ahead of its nearest rival, Cunard, on the competitive transatlantic service between Britain and America. *Olympic* was the first in service of the new fleet, her keel having been laid down in 1908. She was to be a favourite with passengers and crew until she was scrapped in 1935, at which time she was barely seaworthy.

TITANIC

What happens though, when the pride and joy of a fleet of liners hits an iceberg? It fills with water and sinks, regardless of the innovative design that was supposed to stop just such a thing happening. With it went some of the great and good of the day, and many who had strong ties with Southampton.

Looking at the list of the officers and crew of the *Titanic*, it is easy to see how

The Titanic *and the* Olympic *being built.*

the ship's loss affected the port. Although only twenty of the crew were actually born in the port, a further 661 had local addresses. Many of the officers, for example, despite having been born in other areas, had Southampton homes.

The captain, Edward Smith, lived with his family in Winn Road, Portswood. The ship's chief electrician, Peter Sloan, lived at No. 77a Clovelly Road; the chief engineer, Joseph Bell, was living at No. 314 Canute Road; the Senior Second Engineer William Farquharson resided in Wilton Road, Shirley; Norman Harrison, the junior second engineer listed his address as No. 30 Coventry Road. The ship's junior third engineer,

FREDERICK FLEET

Fleet was an experienced lookout, having been on the *Oceanic* in that capacity for four years prior to signing on to the *Titanic's* crew in Belfast. He gave his address then as being No. 9 Norman Road, Southampton.

Fleet had the dubious distinction of being the first to spot the iceberg that sank the ship. He and fellow lookout Reginald Lee did their best to spot obstacles in the ship's path in the pitch black and without binoculars – these had been left behind in Southampton accidently. When he saw the looming mass dead ahead, he gave three pulls on the ship's bell, as was customary, and then reported the iceberg to the Sixth Officer, James Moody. The First Officer, William Murdock, then gave the orders to try to evade the impending disaster.

Fleet helped to load survivors into lifeboat 6 and then was needed to help manage the boat, so survived the sinking of the great ship. He was twenty-four years of age.

Life, so precious when about to be lost, was never to be the same. He served for a time on *Olympic* for the White Star Line but all the crew survivors were to suffer from prejudice – they were seen as unlucky. They were also reminders to the shipping line of a disaster that need not have happened. Fleet resigned from the White Star Line and worked for other shipping lines, including Union-Castle, until 1936 when he gave up working at sea. He then became a shipbuilder for Harland and Wolff and later was Master-at-Arms for the Union-Castle Mail Steamship Company. As an old man, he made his living by selling newspapers in the street in Southampton.

The end of Frederick Fleet's life was tragic. He lost his wife on 28 December 1964. The couple had been living with her brother. Shortly after his sister's death, the brother evicted Fleet. Having lost his wife and his home in rapid succession, Fleet hanged himself. He was seventy-seven years of age. He was buried in a pauper's grave in Hollybrook cemetery in Southampton. His grave was marked with a headstone paid for by The Titanic Historical Society in 1993.

Frederick Fleet.

G. F. Hosking, lived in Avenue Road, Itchen, which became Walpole Road in 1924. Of the crew, some were lucky enough to return, such as William McIntyre from Floating Bridge Road and the ship's lookout, Frederick Fleet, but many more perished. Mess steward John Coleman lived at No. 7 Mortimer Road, Itchen. William Mayo, one of the relatively few victims of the disaster whose body was recovered and given burial at sea, lived at No. 24 Cable Street.

Millbank Street, Northam was one of the many 'Streets of Mourning' (*The Deathless Story of the Titanic*, Lloyd's of London Press Ltd) in the city, where eight houses lost a total of thirteen relatives. As Rance notes, 125 children at Northam Council School had been dependent on relatives lost on the *Titanic*.

Looking at the list of crew on the encyclopaedia-titanica.org website is depressing reading, as the fate of the officers and crew is revealed. A few are listed as rescued from particular lifeboats, some have body numbers assigned to them, which indicates that they were recovered from the freezing water, but the majority are simply listed – their bodies were never found.

The mighty *Titanic* was the second of White Star line's *Olympic* class liners. Mighty was the word. She was 1,000ft long, had four vast funnels, weighed a huge 86,328 tons and from keel to the top of the navigator's bridge was 104ft high. For the time, she was immense.

SPECIAL

She had been built at the Harland and Wolf dockyard in Belfast, her keel being laid in 1909. She was launched in 1911 and members of the public had been invited to inspect the majesty of the ship and marvel at her luxury. Modelled on the five-star Ritz Hotel in London, she boasted a lending library and a barber's shop, while first class passengers could enjoy the gymnasium, swimming pool, and sauna. Third-class passengers enjoyed the novelty of small cabins, rather than the open dormitories provided by other cruise companies for their lower-class clientele. The addition of third-class

smoking and reading areas, open space to promenade on deck and dining rooms added to the general feeling of distinction on the ship. By the time she arrived in Southampton, to pick up passengers for her maiden voyage, the word was out that the *Titanic* was something special.

THE FATEFUL DAY

Titanic left the White Star Dock in Southampton on 10 April 1912, with 1,645 passengers on-board. All was well until she sailed into the history books when she hit an iceberg just four days later. She was 375 miles south of Newfoundland in the North Atlantic. The glancing blow from the iceberg opened four of her sixteen watertight compartments, allowing seawater to rush in. Ironically, if she had not swerved to avoid the ice and had hit it head on, she would probably have stayed afloat.

On board were 2,224 passengers and crew, many from Southampton. One of the passengers was Bruce Joseph Ismay, the chairman of the White Star Line. Survivors of the disaster that followed reported feeling a slight jarring but nothing more to indicate anything had happened. Few passengers strolled out on deck to see what had caused the sensation. Within twenty minutes of

TITANIC MEMORIALS

Southampton abounds with memorials to those who lost their lives on the *Titanic* and there is a heritage trail for those interested in learning more about how the disaster affected the town. The new SeaCity museum at the Civic Centre, opened in time for the centenary of her loss in 2012, offers insights into the ship and her era.

Some of the particular memorials to be seen in Southampton are:

The Titanic Musicians' Memorial

None of the musicians on the ship survived her sinking, so this plaque is particularly poignant. The current memorial is situated on the wall of an office building on the corner of London Road and Cumberland Place. Millvina Dean, the youngest *Titanic* survivor, who was nine weeks old when the disaster occurred, unveiled it in 1990, fifty years after the original memorial was lost in a bombing raid in 1940. The memorial lists the names of all the musicians who died on board the ship. Survivors told of the band continuing to play until the last moment.

The Titanic Musicians' Memorial.

The Titanic Engineer Officers' Memorial

This grand memorial, made of bronze and granite, is Grade II listed and recently restored (2010). It is 30ft high and 20ft wide, and weighs over 60 tons. A winged angel takes centre stage with engineer officers either side, none of whom survived. All the names of the engineer officers on the *Titanic* are listed. Whitehead & Son designed the memorial and over 100,000 came to see it unveiled in 1914.

The Titanic Crew Memorial

This was originally a drinking fountain set outside Southampton Common. It is made of Portland stone cut along classical lines with an urn, four columns and a roof. It was unveiled in 1915 and is a much more modest memorial than that to the Engineer Officers, simply because it took longer to raise the funds from the small means available to the crew's families. The fountain ran into trouble very early on as the common was popular with children. They did not understand its significance and soon were climbing on it or playing with the water, with the result that it had to be fenced off to protect it. The urn was stolen after the Second World War.

The Titanic Engineer Officers' Memorial.

It was moved to the ruins of Holy Rood Church, now a Merchant Navy and Falklands Conflict Memorial, in 1971 and the urn was replaced. The memorial now sits in peace behind an imposing protective fence, next to a speaker point playing the story of the great ship.

the impact, however, the captain knew he was on a doomed vessel and gave the order to abandon ship. Distress flares were sent up and the new Marconi radio was used to broadcast both the CQD distress call (Attention All Stations – Distress or Danger) and the equally new SOS (Save Our Souls) signal. The *Carpathia* was the nearest ship to answer the distress messages. She was four hours away. Unfortunately, the *Titanic* did not have four hours.

Only 705 passengers and crew survived, including Mr Ismay. The ship had hit the iceberg at 11.40, and by 2.20 on the morning of 15 April 1912 she had sunk, broken into two pieces. Many of the lifeboats, of which there were only enough for half of those travelling on the ship, had been launched with few people aboard them. Those in the lifeboats picked up some who were swept into the sea, or who had jumped from the ship, but these were pitifully few. One of these was radio operator Jack Philips, who had remained to the last sending out distress messages. He was alive when recovered but died of hyperthermia soon after. Those in the boats left many survivors to their fate in the water, for fear of overturning. The majority of the survivors were women and children and of these, many were first-class passengers, whose cabins were nearest to the boat deck.

NEWS

News of the sinking of the great ship was met first with disbelief and then shock. The *New York Herald* called the loss of the ship the 'most appalling disaster in maritime history'. Relatives crowded

A group of Titanic *survivors aboard the* Carpathia.

outside the White Star offices at Canute Chambers in Canute Road, anxiously waiting for news. As names and fates became known, the boards were updated. A plaque on the wall now marks the spot where the announcements of those saved and lost were made.

The suffering caused to local families by the *Titanic's* loss was huge. The shipping line stopped pay for those who had died in the disaster and families were faced with the huge costs of transporting bodies back for burial. Many could not afford this and so their loved ones were buried in America, thus denying families the opportunity of closure that a funeral brings. Households had lost their breadwinner and faced mounting hardship. A relief fund was set up in Southampton to help those affected, with fundraising events such as concerts and sports days used to help swell its coffers. The money raised went towards such things as school fees, medical bills, bread and milk. Over 50,000 people turned up for an open-air church service to remember the ship's dead.

The *Titanic* is a ship that will long be remembered, sadly for all the wrong reasons.

MUTINY!

UNDERSTANDABLY, AFTER the disaster that had befallen the *Titanic*, there was a certain amount of trepidation amongst the maritime working community. Was travelling on one of the White Star Line's new liners safe? If the mighty *Titanic* had gone down, might not others of the line do so, too?

MOURNING

The *Olympic* arrived in England soon after the *Titanic*'s loss, on 21 April 1912. The port was in mourning and the ship's owner anxious to restore faith in its liners. The sinking of the *Titanic* had brought to light a number of safety shortfalls and these led, in 1914, to changes in maritime safety laws. Now though, there were immediate changes to the *Olympic* that White Star wanted to implement. There were only three days until the liner was to leave Southampton again, so it was all hands to action to make the safety improvements in the time available. She had a number of new collapsible lifeboats installed. The exact number was to prove a problem. According to Terry Randall on the City of Southampton Society website (www.coss.org.uk/The-Olympic-Mutiny.php), the White Star head office in Liverpool kept changing its mind about the number of new life boats to install, resulting in eleven surplus boats being taken back to dry land. This, to the jittery crew, looked suspiciously as if they had not been passed as safe for use and rumours began to circulate about the safety of the ship.

On the morning of 24 April, Board of Trade Assistant Marine Surveyor at Southampton Captain Maurice Clarke reviewed the new lifeboats, together with the other safety features installed, including the new hands signed on, to make sure that the launching of the boats went smoothly. He put them through their paces and was pleased to put his seal of approval on all the work that had been done in the three-day refit period. The ship could now be made ready to sail.

DESERTERS!

However, just before he could issue sailing clearance, some of the ship's crew, who were not happy with the improved safety measures being taken, had downed tools and deserted the liner. They still considered the ship to be unsafe, as they did not trust the collapsible lifeboats the ship had been fitted with. There was no discussing the matter. New crewmembers had to be found, and found fast.

While the ship waited off Spithead for the replacement men to be recruited, Captain Clarke put the new lifeboat drills to the test again. This time, it took far longer for the boats to be lowered – a worrying two hours compared to twelve-and-a-half minutes when tested earlier. Later, when union officials sent to negotiate the dispute asked for a representative sample of boats to be lowered into the water and left for two hours, it was seen that one of the six boats that were tested was not watertight. It had a small hole in it. This gave credence to the deserters' safety claims. The union agreed to recommend that the ship was safe, provided that the faulty boat was replaced.

When 168 new crewmembers finally arrived, late in the evening of 25 April, it looked as if the ship could depart at last. However, it was not long before more of the *Olympic*'s crew flagged up safety concerns. This time the problem was the quality of the new crew. Many of the men brought aboard were not seamen but miners, used to coal shovelling; although this would be their job on the voyage, they were not used to life at sea. They were also not union men, which was a major part of the problem.

The *Olympic*'s captain, James Haddock, ordered the men back to their duties, but did so in vain. The men simply did not have faith in the new crew and refused to work with them. At the end of his patience, Captain Haddock eventually had to call in the Royal Navy to arrest fifty-three men, who were later tried for mutiny in Portsmouth. Another crew was hastily recruited but most of these were found to be unfit for their duties and so it was no surprise to hear, on 26 April, that the voyage was cancelled.

Non-union labour was brought in to replace the firemen in the engine room, keeping the ship's coal engines stoked, and, on 15 May 1912, the *Olympic* finally sailed to New York.

The whole episode was a sorry tale for the White Star Line, made worse when the mutineers were found guilty of wilful disobedience of the captain's orders on 5 May, but no penalty was imposed. By then, the shipping line was also facing an enquiry into the loss of the *Titanic* ...

The launch of the Olympic.

1937

SOUTHAMPTON AND THE SPANISH CIVIL WAR

HORROR

The awful aftermath of the bombing of Guernica, subject of one of Picasso's most famous works, brought the horrors of modern warfare home to the people of Southampton three years before they were to experience it for themselves.

In May 1927, Southampton welcomed refugees from the Basque region – 4,000 Spanish children, fleeing the carnage. They arrived on board the liner *Habana* and brought with them tales of the devastation that made those that heard them shudder.

BOMBING

Monday 26 April 1937 was market day in the former Basque region capital. At 3.45 in the afternoon the first German aeroplane – belonging to Condor Legion and set up specifically to fight on the side of Franco's Nationalist rebel forces against the elected government – took off to bomb Guernica. The resulting carnage and the destruction of the town was a lesson to the Germans of how devastating to morale blanket bombing of a civilian town – a new strategy – could be.

CAMP

The children were sheltered in tents set up in a huge camp in North Stoneham. The camp was organised by the National Joint Committee for Spanish Relief, which had branches up and down the country, and trade union members from Southampton erected the tents. The children were later relocated to West End and other centres. By 1939 most had returned to Spain, but 250 were still in Southampton in 1945. Many stayed to take up permanent residence in the town.

Left *Guernica after the German raids.*

SEPTEMBER 1940

THE SUPERMARINE RAIDS

IT TOOK THE Luftwaffe three attempts to hit the Supermarine works along the River Itchen at Woolston. Each of the daylight raids cost Southampton civilian lives and hundreds of homes and other buildings.

The problem, as far as Southampton was concerned, was the proximity to each other of strategic aspects of the UK's war effort. Supermarine had two sites close to each other on the river's edge. Here was the home of R. J. Mitchell's proud baby, the Spitfire.

Vosper Thorneycroft was a close neighbour, a busy naval shipyard. In the area was everything that one would expect to be associated with such enterprises. Nearby were residential streets. What was Southampton's problem, however, was the Luftwaffe's joy. With so much of such importance situated so neatly together, it should have been a doddle to knock the lot off in one swift and deadly swipe. That it took three attempts meant that the destruction in the area was immense, as bombs missed their targets and hit other areas.

There had been a raid on Eastleigh aerodrome on 11 September, in which about fifty people had been killed in an attack that was meant to destroy the Spitfire flight unit there but which hit the Cunliffe-Owen factory next door instead. However, thirty-four houses were completely destroyed and over 1,000 others were damaged in the first full raid on the river industries, on 15 September. Twelve tons of explosives rained down and the damage was to such an extent that the ruins of the homes left behind were used for training soldiers in the run up to D-Day. Six people died that day in a raid that was totally off its mark. The Supermarine works suffered only from broken windows.

The second raid was not unexpected, given the misses of the 15 September, but in the event, the raiders arrived before the air raid sirens had had time to give the alert. On 24 September thirty-seven bombers swooped down and unleashed havoc on Southampton. By the end of the raid, forty-two people were dead and over 170 were injured. Many people died during their flight from the Supermarine site in Itchen, either when they were caught under an archway beneath the railway line when it collapsed on top of them, following a direct hit, or when the shelter they were in also received a direct hit. From all of this, the Supermarine site in Woolston received only minor damage, although there was more serious damage done to a railway bridge, which was

On Thursday 19 April 2012, Fox News reported that up to twenty Second World War era Rolls Royce Griffon-powered Spitfire aeroplanes had been found buried in crates in Burma.

They had been shipped in 1945, two years before production ceased – waxed, wrapped in greased paper and then tarred as protection against the elements. They were found to be surplus to requirements and so, in order that they did not fall into enemy hands, they were buried in their delivery crates.

British farmer David Cundall, a sixty-two-year-old aviation enthusiast, spent fifteen years and $200,000 (about £124,000) searching for the lost planes. Having located the site of the burial, being kept secret at the time of the report, he sent a camera down a borehole to see the machines. 'They seemed to be in good condition,' he is quoted as saying. In February 2013, plans to dig the site halted as it appeared that the Spitfires believed buried there were a 'myth' (BBC News). Another site is now being considered. Of the more than 20,000 manufactured, there are only about thirty-five still flying worldwide.

destroyed. Given that this raid, too, had not achieved its aim, the staff and local population braced itself for a third raid.

This was not long in coming. It was vital to the German war effort to put as much out of business along the River Itchen as it could, and Luftwaffe command was determined to do just that. At 4.30 that afternoon on 26 September 1940, 120 aircraft filled the skies above Woolston once again. Blanket bombing was the order of the day and both sides of

Mitchell's baby, the Spitfire, came to fire the public's imagination. Supermarine had two sites on the River Itchen at Woolston.

the river were the targets. Seventy tons of explosives rained down on the area. This tactic was more successful. Seven bombs hit the Woolston Supermarine site and one landed on the Itchen site, inflicting damage on Spitfire fuselages being assembled there. Fifty-five people were killed in the raid and ninety-four were hurt. On the far side of the riverbank in Chapel, the raids produced appalling tales of loss as air raid shelters and private homes were hit.

After the third raid, the complete dispersal of Supermarine was ordered and sections of its work were transferred all over Southampton and surrounding areas. Management teams were housed in the Polygon Hotel and manufacturing was split between sites with nearby aerodromes as far afield as Reading, Trowbridge and Salisbury. Up until the Woolston and Itchen sites were destroyed, there had been 1,198 Spitfires delivered to the RAF from Supermarine. During the dispersal of the works this dipped to 350 delivered. Overall, by VE Day a stunning 7,327 Spitfires had been received (Russell, 1994). Although the raids undoubtedly dented Spitfire production, it continued. That, as far as Britain was concerned, was the main thing.

THE BOMBING OF THE SCHOOL OF ART, CIVIC CENTRE

SOUTHAMPTON SUFFERED FIFTY-SEVEN air raid attacks and over 1,500 air raid warnings during the Second World War. The port was vital to Britain's war effort and Hitler knew it. The main targets were the Supermarine factory in Woolston and the docks, but it was the civilians living in the town that took the brunt of the more than 470 tons of explosives dropped on Southampton (plimsoll.org). Hitler was determined to undermine morale in the city, too.

Of the many heartbreaking stories in Southampton's bloody history, it is the bombing of the Civic Centre building by the German Luftwaffe, on 6 November 1940, that is one of the most keenly remembered.

On that fateful day, children were working in the School of Art, part of the eighteen-month-old Art Gallery. There had been several false air raid alarms and so, when the alarm was sounded once more at just before 2.45 that afternoon, not everyone went into the basement designated as the bomb shelter for the site. Those who did not get to the basement and tried to get to its shelter later, were forced back by the scale of the rubble from the roof and floors that the bomb had ripped through, and by the noise of screaming from behind the impenetrable barricade.

The basement had not been given any extra protection with its designation. It was simply the area under the building, the furthest away from the street level. It held central heating pipes, full of boiling hot water.

Children from the Central District Girls' School, all aged between eleven and thirteen years, had been busy sewing. They just had time to scramble to the basement when the art school was hit by one of twelve 500lb bombs dropped on the Civic Centre area. They were described as a 'ladder falling' rather than separate bombs by Mrs Grace Lloyd, a witness to the carnage.

CATASTROPHIC

The results were catastrophic, as Andrew Bissell relates in his book *Southampton's Children of the Blitz* (2001). The bomb destroyed all in its path and exploded in the basement, killing fourteen children from the school. Of those trapped in the basement, many were scalded when the heating pipes burst, showering them with boiling water. Only one of the party from the Central District Girl's' School lived to tell the tale. She was thirteen-

The School of Art in the Civic Centre was bombed on 6 November 1940. Lacking proper air raid shelters, children taking an art class at the time of the air raid were directed to the basement, which received a direct hit.

year-old Audrey Hunt, from Northbrook Road. She spoke later of her memories of the incident. A 'big thud' was heard and she could see the sky above her. Contemporary photographs show the whole of the front of the building to be missing. Audrey remembered the 'noise and screaming all around me.'

In and around the Civic Centre, the blast, fire and smoke claimed twenty-one further casualties and many more were injured.

Bodies were taken to the Royal South Hants hospital and family members had the unenviable task of identifying the dead. As the sister of one of the basement victims explained, this was difficult as they were 'burnt to a cinder.'

Sadly, the bombing of the School of Art was not the last example of Hitler's war on the local population. The worst was still to come ...

1944

D-DAY

MISERY

The world had never seen anything like the Second World War. After the awfulness of the First World War, everyone hoped that they would never experience the like again. They did not – it was worse in many ways, simply because this time around memories still reached back to gas attacks, trenches and misery, and fear was added to the mix.

A GIFT!

Southampton was vital to the war effort. As in countless other conflicts, the port was used as an embarkation point for troops going off to fight, and for bringing back the sick and injured. It was also a logistics point, sending off the supplies that kept the men fighting. The reason for this was the wonderful gift nature had bestowed on Southampton Water – its double high tide. This meant that it was the only port in the land that could be used by large vessels at any stage of the tide. Perfect!

Southampton and its immediate environs were fully exploited throughout the war years: American troops busily guarded prisoners of war in transit camps on what is now the retail park beside IKEA, munitions were manufactured

and the docks fully employed. By 1944, it was gearing up to play its biggest part yet for two years. To do so, it had had to get over the effects of the Southampton Blitz in 1940. Operation Overlord, the invasion of Europe, was about to begin and Southampton was to have a major role in making it happen and to keep the military wheels turning.

The 375 acres of Southampton Common were ideal as marshalling areas for troops because the wooded landscape concealed them from prying eyes flying overhead. It was also within easy reach of the docks the troops would embark from. Other sites within a twelve-mile arc of the port were also earmarked; from just outside Winchester through Romsey and Chandlers Ford to Swaything, and a huge amount of infrastructure was installed. New roads, depots and slipways were built, together with such essentials as fuel dumps and security camps. All was made ready to cope with the thousands of troops destined to pass through Southampton, and all their supplies that came with them.

In July 1943, a trial run of the area was held, to see if Southampton could cope with what was expected of it. Thousands of troops were bussed in and transited through the docks. From this dummy run, which many of the locals in the town thought was for real and so turned out en masse to wave the men off, much useful information was learnt. Most importantly, it was found that a massive 11,000 troops could be embarked on each tide. As there were four tides every twenty-four hours, this meant that 44,000 troops could be passed through the docks in a day. More infrastructure was later added, so that when the troops left for real, on 6 June 1944, the numbers leaving each day were 53,750, along with 7,070 vehicles (Ford, *Hampshire and D-Day*).

A landing craft at Omaha Beach.

The Southampton dockworkers joined civilian companies all over England in helping to build Mulberry harbour sections, which were vital to the force's ability to land and supply themselves in France because the enemy occupied every port. These were huge floating components, which fitted together like a jigsaw puzzle to form a safe harbour for men and equipment acting as reinforcements to be landed onto the Normandy beaches.

Two of the artificial harbours were built at Arromanches and along the French coastline of three villages: Sainte-Honorine-des-Pertes, Saint-Laurent-sur-Mer and Vierville-sur-Mer. These three were jointly codenamed Omaha Beach. The Mulberry harbours, the size of Dover and built in just two weeks, were towed out by tugs and assembled off the beaches after old scrap ships had been scuttled to form a breakwater. By 9 June, both the Mulberry Harbours were complete, with 33 jetties and ten miles of floating roads apiece. However, the harbour at Omaha Beach was destroyed

---

The influx of American soldiers into Southampton must have seemed like a dream come true to children during the war. The GIs had in abundance what had been strictly rationed in Britain since 1940: sugar, or more specifically, sweets and gum. Kids soon caught on and the question, 'Got any gum, Chum?' would be politely flung at passing American soldiers in the hope of striking it lucky. The Americans had soon cottoned on and were usually happy to oblige. The phrase inspired a jazz song written by Murray Kane in 1944.

James Marsh, in his 2011 biography *Growing Up in Wartime Southampton – Other People's Trousers,* recalls hearing troop trains on the railway line at the bottom of his garden in Belgrave Road and, with the other kids of the area, rushing to the line to wave at the soldiers and pick up the sweets and other items thrown out of the carriage windows for them by the soldiers.

Iris Mardon was born in 1939. She has vivid memories of wartime Southampton.

My parents had a cafe on the Western Esplanade Southampton, opposite the Lido swimming baths. I well remember mum carrying me to the air raid shelter on nights when the sirens sounded. It was situated on the pavement just outside our home. It was dimly lit. It served my family and several other families in that part of the street. I seem to remember people just chatting to each other passing the time of day, maybe a singsong or two. I think I may have slept through a lot of it. From our windows, we could see the barrage balloons flying over the docks.

One cottage down the road from us was totally destroyed. All that was left was the garden where my brother and I would go and pick the flowers. I can still remember watching from the window the Pirelli factory ablaze; the fire was put out and the building lived on.

My brother was older than me. One day when he was on his way home, the siren sounded, my brother could hear aircraft overhead and he had the presence of mind to get under a parked vehicle for safety.

On another occasion, dad found a piece of shrapnel in the back garden. It was the shape of the letter Y with grooves along it; the letter B was circled on it. Dad's name being Bert, he always said it was meant for him.

I only saw the aftermath of the bombing when out shopping with mum. The High Street, Above and Below Bar were badly hit. Woolworths had the top of the building destroyed; only the basement was open for business. St Mary's Street was spared from bombing, there you could buy most things.

I have very clear memories of the build-up to D-Day, but of course we did not know about D-Day at that time. Days and days before June 6th 1944 convoys of trucks, tanks, amphibious vehicles and British and American troops passed by our home on their way to the docks to board ships and landing craft for the invasion. I would stand on the pavement outside my dad's cafe waving to the troops as they passed by, very often being thrown sweets and chocolate bars from the American soldiers.

At the end of the war, I joined in the dancing and singing in the Rose Garden near the Civic Centre on VE day 1945.

by a storm on 19 June, leaving the Arromanches harbour to do all the work. The Mulberry Harbours were designed to operate for ninety days, but in the event, the single survivor continued for more than six months before it was no longer needed and abandoned. Its remnants can still be seen today.

After D-Day, Southampton continued to supply the troops and so its role continued unabated to the end of the war. Alastair Arnott, in *Maritime Southampton* sums up the contribution Southampton made to the war effort in the final year of the Second World War. From the beginning of Operation Overload on 6 June 1944 – when the men left Britain – to May 1945, the port handled a staggering 2,840,346 troops; 257,580 vehicles; 20,516 railway wagons; 770 locomotives; 39 ambulance wagons; 22 breakdown trains and 16 mobile workshops.

1830-1965

THE COLISEUM

IT IS HARD to believe now that one of Southampton's biggest and brightest lights has been almost completely forgotten. Indeed, were it not for the efforts of local historian Pam Whittington in alerting the author to the building, it would not have made it into this book. The Local Studies Desk at Southampton Reference Library thankfully has some references and cuttings that go some way to bringing the place alive once more.

Set in the heart of what was once Southampton's glittering entertainment district, the Coliseum in Portland Terrace was originally built in about 1830 to house the Victoria Skating Rink.

By about 1880, the building was a large corrugated iron structure, the brainchild of Jonas Nichols, the local Justice of the Peace and councillor who gave his name to Nicholstown.

This was replaced just before the First World War with a magnificent edifice: the Coliseum. At 12,000 square feet, it was big enough to hold political rallies, sporting events and shows. Famous names appearing there included singer Clare Butt, billiards players Joe Davis and Claude Falkiner, and up-and-coming politicians such as the young Anthony Eden.

SCANDAL

In 1918, Dr Marie Stopes (1880–1958) had published *Married Love or Love in Marriage*. Several influential publishers turned down this book because of its content. Eventually published, it soon sold out and ran to several editions in the first year. Dr Stopes had the courage to put in writing the observation that women's sexual desire coincides with ovulation and the time period before menstruation. She also advocated an equal relationship between marriage partners. The book caused outrage in the UK, and was banned in the USA as obscene until 1931.

Dr Stopes and her husband Verdon Roe, with whom she set up the first birth control clinic in the UK in 1921, came to Southampton in about 1925. She gave a lecture at the Coliseum, which was attended by Lavinia C. Witt from Bitterne. In a letter to the *Southampton Daily Echo* in September 1965 she says she heard Dr Stokes speak, 'on the subject of 'Birth Control' – at that time a subject surrounded by a great deal of secrecy, not even discussed by 'nice' people and certainly not from a public platform ... the hall was full (seating capacity was 1,600, I think) and they had all paid their 2/6 to come in.'

PUNCH HIS LIGHTS OUT!

The Coliseum was used for a particularly bloody sport: boxing. Looking at the list of Hampshire's boxers, available on the nipperpatdaly.co.uk website, it is startling to see how many were from Southampton. The brothers George and Joe Beckett, for example, are credited with seventeen and fifty-nine fights respectively in the 1910s and '20s. They are mentioned in John J. Shaw's letter to the *Echo* in 1976. He recalls boxers such as the aptly titled Punch, who had twenty-three bouts during the same era as the Becketts. Alfred Clinton of Bassett remembers Seaman Gregory, who had eight recorded fights during the 1910s, in his letter to the newspaper in September 1976.

SECOND WORLD WAR

In 1939, the Coliseum was used as a GPO telephone exchange. Pam Whittington says, 'I was a GPO telephonist in the old Coliseum and about fifteen at the time ... It was a strict environment, for mostly women and girls, but men came in to work the night shifts.

'One telephonist was Queenie Smith. She was a relation of my stepfather's. She received an award, possibly the MBE, for staying at her switchboard whilst heavy bombing was taking place around her.'

The end of an era came for the Coliseum in 1965. It was knocked down to make way for the new Inner Ring Road. The telephone exchange was moved to a purpose-built site in Ogle Road and soon, collective memory began to dim as the Coliseum's glittering past faded into obscurity.

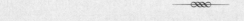

Pam Whittington retains one vivid memory of her time working at the Coliseum.

In Spa Road, adjacent to the Portland Terrace, where the Coliseum was situated, there was an abattoir. William Passey owned the Hants Abattoir Ltd. It was there in 1927 until 1945. One of the worst aspects of this placing was when an animal would make a break for freedom, roaring and running as men shouted and chased after it. It was a chilling happening and one that stayed in the memories of the girls who heard the sad noises, because, needless to say, the wretched animal was always caught and brought back to its fate.

BIBLIOGRAPHY

BOOKS

Arnott, A., *Maritime Southampton* (Derby: Breedon Books, 2002)

Bissell, A., *Southampton's Children of the Blitz* (Bournemouth: Red Post Books, 2001)

Brown, J., *Southampton Murder Victims* (Derby: Derby Books, 2010)

Davies, Rev. J. S., *A History of Southampton* (Southampton: Gilbert & Co.; London: Hamilton, Adams & Co., 1883)

Doughty, M., (Ed.) *Hampshire and D-Day* (Hampshire Books, 1994)

Eddleston, J. J., *Foul Deeds and Suspicious Deaths in and Around Southampton* (Barnsley: Pen and Sword Books, 2009)

Evans, I., (Ed.) *Brewer's Dictionary of Phrase and Fable 14th Edition* (London: Cassell Publishers Ltd., 1990)

Hanna, R., *London Literature, 1300-1380* (Cambridge University Press, 2005)

Jones, T. B., *Hampshire Papers: The Black Death in Hampshire* (Hampshire County Council, 1999)

Legg, P., *Southampton Then & Now* (Stroud: The History Press, 2010)

Leonard, A. G. K., *More Stories of Southampton Streets* (Paul Cave Publications Ltd, 1989)

Marsh, J., *Growing Up in Wartime Southampton: Other People's Trousers* (Stroud: The History Press, 2011)

Moody, B., *150 Years of Southampton Docks* (Kingfisher Railway Productions, Southampton, 1988)

Rance, A., *Southampton: An Illustrated History* (Milestone Publications in association with the City of Southampton, 1986)

Rance, A., *Shipbuilding in Victorian Southampton* (Southampton University Industrial Archaeology Group, 1981)

Rance, A., *A Victorian Photographer in Southampton* (Southampton: Paul Cave Publications Ltd, 1980)

Rance, A., *Southampton and its Museums* (Southampton: Paul Cave Publications Ltd, 1980)

Russell, C. R., *Spitfire Postscript*, (C. R. Russell, 1994)

Shore, T. W., *History of Hampshire* (Elliot Stock, 1892, EP Publishing Edition, 1976)

Sly, N., *More Hampshire Murders* (Stroud: The History Press, 2010)

Turner, J. M. W., Cooke, W. B. & Cooke, G., *Picturesque Views on the Southern Coast of England* (John & Arthur Arch, Cornhill, 1826)

Whitelock, D, (Ed) et al., *The Anglo-Saxon Chronicle* (London: Eyre and Spottiswoode, 1961)

PAPERS

Spicer, A., 'The French-speaking Reformed community and their Church in Southampton 1567-*c.* 1620'. (Unpublished Ph.D. thesis, University of Southampton,1994 on http://sohier.free.fr/southamptongb.htm)

Turner, V., 'Legends, Lions, and Virgins: The Legend of Sir Bevois of Southampton' (published 2001 on www.southernlife.org.uk)

NEWSPAPERS

Southampton Daily Echo

WEBSITES

www.archive.org
www.arundelcastle.org
www.basquechildren.org
www.bbc.co.uk
www.bitterne.net
www.britarch.ac.uk
www.british-civil-wars.co.uk
www.british-history.ac.uk
www.castles.me.uk
www.dailyecho.co.uk
www.ebooksread.com
www.encyclopedia-titanica.org
www.freepages.genealogy.rootsweb.ancestry.
  com
www.gatehouse-gazetteer.info
www.h2g2.com
www.heritage-history.com
www.history.com
www.inventors.about.com
www.jakesimpkin.org
www.jakesimpkin.org
www.libraryireland.com
www.livingstoneonline.ucl.ac.uk
www.localhistories.org
www.luminarium.org
www.mayoclinic.com
www.medicinenet.com
www.nationalarchives.gov.uk

www.newadvent.org
www.nipperpatdaly.co.uk
www.india.nydailynews.com
www.oxforddnb.com
www.plimsoll.org
www.peartreechurch.org.uk
www.perdurabo10.tripod.com
www.phrases.org.uk
www.plymouthdata.info
www.richardiii.net
www.richardiii.net
www.scrollpublishing.com
www.snopes.com
www.southampton.gov.uk
www.southampton.gov.uk
www.sotoncitycentreparish.hampshire.org.uk
www.southampton.ac.uk
www.southampton-music.info
www.southernlife.org.uk
www.spartacus.schoolnet.co.uk
www.themcs.org
www.truecrimelibrary.com
www.unionhistory.info
www.usatoday30.usatoday.com
www.warsoftheroses.com
www.westminster-abbey.org
www.wiki.answers.com
www.en.wikipedia.org
www.winchelsea.net
www.youtube.com